3⁰⁰

W9-CHN-171

THE WOODWORKER'S BOOK OF WOODEN TOYS

When I am grown to man's estate,
I shall be very proud and great,
And tell the other girls and boys,
Not to meddle with my toys.

Robert Louis Stevenson

An early seventeenth-century wood engraving depicting a child at play with his hobbyhorse and a crudely improvised windmill. Courtesy of Victoria and Albert Museum, London.

THE WOODWORKER'S BOOK OF WOODEN TOYS

How to Make Toys That Whirr, Bob, and Make Musical Sounds

Vance Studley

VAN NOSTRAND REINHOLD COMPANY
New York Cincinnati Toronto London Melbourne

Other books by Vance Studley:

Making Artist's Tools
Calligraphy: Appreciation and Form
The Art and Craft of Handmade Paper
Left-Handed Calligraphy

Copyright © 1980 by Litton Educational Publishing, Inc.
Library of Congress Catalog Card Number 79-20405
ISBN 0-442-27919-1

All rights reserved. No part of this work covered by the copyright
hereon may be reproduced or used in any form or by any means—
graphic, electronic, or mechanical, including photocopying, record-
ing, taping, or information storage and retrieval systems—without
written permission of the publisher.

Printed in the United States of America
Designed by Loudan Enterprises

Published by Van Nostrand Reinhold Company
A division of Litton Educational Publishing, Inc.
135 West 50th Street, New York, NY 10020, U.S.A.

Van Nostrand Reinhold Limited
1410 Birchmount Road
Scarborough, Ontario M1P 2E7, Canada

Van Nostrand Reinhold Australia Pty. Ltd.
17 Queen Street
Mitcham, Victoria 3132, Australia

Van Nostrand Reinhold Company Limited
Molly Millars Lane
Wokingham, Berkshire, England

16 15 14 13 12 11 10 9 8 7 6 5 4 3 2

Library of Congress Cataloging in Publication Data

Studley, Vance.
The woodworker's book of wooden toys.

1. Wooden toy making. I. Title.
TTI174.5.W6S78   745.59'2   79-20405
ISBN 0-442-27919-1

Dedicated to my son, Tyler,
who can, regardless of material, make a
toy out of anything.

Acknowledgments

For their help in the preparation of this book I am sincerely indebted to the many people and organizations who unstintingly gaye their time and talents. I wish to extend my deepest gratitude to Chris Krake for his visual contributions; Garabed Mardirossian; Sue Mossman; Margo Studley; U.S. Department of Agriculture Forest Products Laboratory; Miss E. M. Aslin, Keeper of the Bethnal Green Museum of Childhood; the British Museum; The Huntington Library; and the trustees of the Victoria and Albert Museum.

Special thanks to my many students who allowed me to reproduce some of the examples of their work pictured in this book and made toy design as enjoyable as toy play.

CONTENTS

FOREWORD

Carefully wrap the taut, braided string around the base of the wooden top. Slip the loop on the opposite end of the string over your finger; pull tight. Hold the top, half encircled with precise and even rows of string, in your best throwing hand. Quickly, without hesitation, pitch the top in front of you with a sidewinding twist and watch it spinning madly—a whirling dervish of form, softly humming as it moves, skating freely with no appointed place to go. This is no object for a glass case of rare and precious things; it was made to be used. Its beauty is enhanced by its feel and its function.

As a child grows and develops, so does the sophistication of his playthings and his use of them. A baby will happily chew on a block, a two-year-old will stack it on top of others, a five-year-old will build elaborate constructions, realistic or fantastic. Once a child has developed even minimal skills, he no longer waits for toys to come his way. He fashions his own from straws, cardboard, paper, wire, scraps of wood, bits of plastic, metal cans, colored yarn, and an inordinate amount of glue and other sticky stuff. Half, if not more, of the fun is in the making of these inventions. So, too, for the craftsman, there is enjoyment in the processes of his craft, not only in the end result.

The wooden toys in this book were chosen because they provide joy in their making as well as in their being. The selecting of the wood, the arranging, shaping, assembling and finishing of it, all yield a certain satisfaction to the woodworker. The use of rare and exotic woods is suggested because their beauty and individuality will add a dimension to the finished toy, but also because each offers a unique experience for the woodcrafter.

The purpose of this book is to free the creative instincts in all of us, to salvage the wonder of toys and their construction from childhoods past.

INTRODUCTION

Toys, like other household items, have a long history that has taken many curious turns along the way. It was long thought that the earliest playthings dated back to Egyptian times. However, recent finds in the Nile valley have clearly been antedated by objects found in excavations on the Indian subcontinent. The earliest objects made for play were composed of natural materials. Rattles and balls were made from dried gourds, and birds or other animals were fashioned from fiber, dried grass, nuts, bark, bone fragments, and strips of leather.

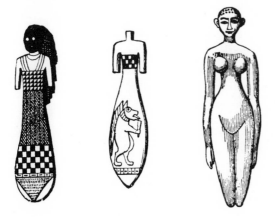

Figure 1.
The basis for the spinning top—one of the most universal toys—originated in primitive man's attempt to spin a crudely made, hand-hewn rock.

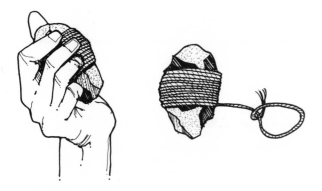

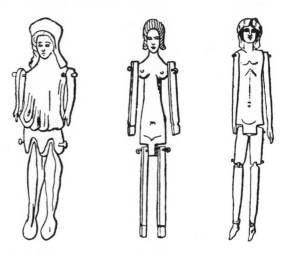

Figure 2.
Drawing of early Egyptian, Greek, and Roman dolls. Dolls of this sort were made to divert children and keep them occupied while household activities went on. Often painted, the later versions of these dolls were made with jointed arms and legs. The heads of the Greek dolls were well modeled with hair arranged in true Grecian style. The bodies were proportioned following the ideal human form.

These early toys are divided into two categories—toys proper and toys votive (those made for magical or religious purposes). It has been suggested by historians that, throughout history, when a votive object, such as a shrine doll or idol, ceased to have religious value, it fell into the hands of children to become a plaything. This may well explain the very origins of toys themselves. It does seem likely that toy noisemakers, such as clapper wheels and whistles, whirring devices, and toys designed for crude movement, are derived from objects once used by priests and worshippers as part of ritual belief. It is known, for example, that the first water-bubbling bird whistle was invented over one century before the birth of Christ by Hero, a priestess of Aphrodite.

Figure 3.
Drawing of an early alligator toy made of wood. The jaw of this toy was made movable by a simple jointed mechanism. It seems that animals have been common playthings among children for a long time. This model dates back to 1100 B.C.

Figure 4.
Drawing of a saber-toothed tiger made of wood. The lower jaw moves by means of a wire attachment. This toy dates back to 200 B.C.

Figure 5.
Woodcut of the fifteenth century, depicting what authorities take to be doll makers at their craft. Wood-cut by Hortus Sanitatis.

Figure 6.
*A sixteenth-century woodcut depicting "the games of
Emperor Maximilian." The sixteenth century brought
with it an ever increasing demand for handmade toys.
Paintings of that time, such as the famous* Kinderspel *by
Brueghel, show children at play with ball and bat, cup
and ball, and other toys. Later in the century, trained
craftsmen were retained by the upper classes to fashion
exquisite animals in fine wood or precious stones,
soldiers in silver and gold, and, most notably, miniature
copies of domestic and kitchen articles for dollhouses.
Woodcut by Hans Burgkmair, 1516.*

Figure 7.
Children at the Dresden Market. Germany took the lead in the making of popular toys in the nineteenth century. As more ingenious manufacturing techniques became available, mechanical toys came of age. By the end of the century the manufacturing of these toys had become one of Germany's most important industries, the center of which was in Nuremberg.

Drawing by Ludwig Richter, circa 1850. Original in the Kupferstichkabinett, Dresden.

In more recent times, during the past four centuries, dolls and other toys have been made from wax, papier-mâché, rubber, and porcelain. After World War I, new materials came into use, such as artificial hides, cotton and worsted fabrics, celluloid, tin, and lightweight metals. The period after World War II brought additional refinements, novelties in design, and an entire new range of plastic playthings. Plastic remains the most popular toy-making material in the world today because of its great versatility.

Figure 9.
A cast-iron toy of the early nineteenth century. Cast iron, not widely used by American manufacturers until the late nineteenth century, was applied to practically all forms of figures, from animals to horse-drawn vehicles such as this one.

Figure 8.
The manufacturing of tin toys took an especially large leap in the United States after the Civil War and became tremendously popular after World War I. Inexpensive and easy to manage, tin was an ideal material from which toys could be mass-produced. Shown here is a tin bus made in Poland.

Figure 10.
Drawing of a typical toy soldier. Toy soldiers, whether of wood or metal, have long been a favorite toy among young and old. Terra-cotta horsemen of ancient Greece and Rome were the forerunners of the medieval toy soldiers. The ancient soldiers were made of silver or gold and were the pride of noble households. Eventually, soldiers of solid lead were perfected by the German toy industry. Hand-cast soldiers made with exacting detail were subsequently invented and developed in London.

a

b

c

Yet, the toy that is pieced and fitted by the human hand has a beauty that is simply an inherent part of it, like the fragrance and color of a flower. It is inseparable from its function. It is a beautiful thing because it is a useful thing. Many of the toys that find their way into our museums and private collections once belonged to a culture in which beauty was not an isolated and autonomous value, but a part of everyday life. Household items produced by hand bore the metaphorical fingerprints of the artisan who fashioned them.

Figure 11–a, b, and c.
Ever-increasing realism came about as a result of new working techniques. Craftsmen continued to refine toy objects to further bring about realism as these examples depict: a) A push-along horse made in England at the end of the nineteenth century. b) A wooden horse, crude in appearance, yet highly accurate in its detailed method of construction. c) A rocking horse, stylized in the tradition of late nineteenth century English rocking horses. Courtesy of Victoria and Albert Museum, London.

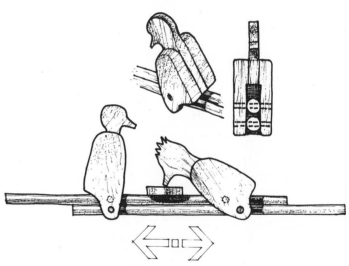

Figure 12.
Drawing of the pecking birds toy, which is activated by two narrow strips of wood moving back and forth to bring the heads down in a tapping fashion. Toys that move, originating in the string-manipulated animals of ancient Egypt, have always been favorites.

Figure 13.
The pecking bird principle applied to two wood-carvers.

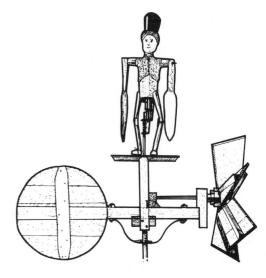

Figure 15.
A more complex whirligig involving a paddle and propellers.

Figure 14.
Drawing of an eighteenth-century whirligig, "sailor Jack." Whirligigs were architectural carvings that developed during the colonial period in the United States. They were chiefly decorative devices activated by strong wind. The function of the weather vane was to indicate wind directions. It was often made by untrained, amateur carvers. Both whirligigs and weather vanes make up a characteristic phase of American folk art.

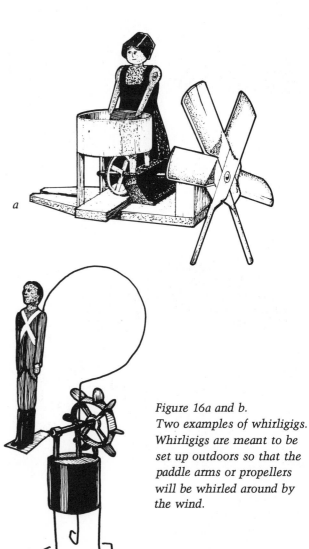

Figure 16a and b.
Two examples of whirligigs. Whirligigs are meant to be set up outdoors so that the paddle arms or propellers will be whirled around by the wind.

Figure 17.
Drawing of a wooden push-pull toy. A push or pull in either direction will produce a delightful Ferris-wheel motion.

Wood and its role in toy making have a long tradition. One of the more easily worked materials and one of the most beautiful and versatile, wood holds a time-honored position as an ideal raw material. Originally, spruce and larch were used for cheap toys; lime, beech, and ash for carved models; and boxwood for items to be faced with a great deal of wear. American wood toys of earlier days were strong and robust. Wagons, sledges, building blocks, and ships were common; toy guns were made from hollow elder branches, kites from supple hazel, and fishing rods from ash with tips of lancewood. The toys presented here are meant to follow in this tradition while, at the same time, utilizing the magnificent array of exotic woods not available to earlier toy makers.

Many of the toys in this book are extensions of toys you probably made as a child. The only requirement here is that you place a few hand tools and several pieces of special woods at your disposal. Unlike many of the toy-making books on the shelves, this book goes beyond the commonplace by virtue of the toys' functions and the particular woods used in their making. Some proficiency with woodworking is helpful, but not required.

For the person wishing to review some of the basics, a section of the book provides a description of the tools by name and function. Also included is a listing and description of many of the woods that are available to the craftsman and some pointers on how to choose and employ these woods in your toy-making ventures. The sections on tools and glues and adhesives will answer some of your questions about their selection and use.

The enjoyment you find in making these toys will add to the pleasure you will have in using them yourself and watching others play with them. Toys are not just for children. They are for anyone who wants to have fun.

Figure 18.
A hollowed-out piece of hardwood was used to make this simple toy whistle.

Figure 19.
As they mature, children become preoccupied with miscellaneous gadgets, which invite a more in-depth study of the objects and experiences in the grown-up world.

15

WOODS FOR TOY MAKING

Wood is the most variable and adaptable raw material available and is used for a wide range of purposes. Modern technology has made available many alternatives, from plastics and metals to concrete and earthenware, yet timber continues to hold its own. Each and every piece of wood you choose for your toy-making project brings with it a hint of the faraway forest where it grew. The rainfall that nurtured it, the condition of the soil, the movement of the sun, the amount of light it received, the proximity of surrounding trees, its preparation by the woodsman's ax, and the subsequent milling; all these features contribute to the ultimate transformation of a once living tree into an object we use and treasure.

Though hard and durable enough for everyday wear and abuse, wood is somehow sympathetic to our needs, especially in the toy-making process. It does not present the sharp or harsh edges of metal, glass, or concrete, and,

Figure I–2.
The wood you select for your toy can often exhibit interesting grain and contrasting colors, all a part of wood's natural characteristics.

Figure I–1.
Inlaid pieces of wood give this box the appearance of geometric detail and illustrate that wood is capable of providing surface richness not unlike its jeweled counterparts.

Figure I–3.
When sawn, sanded, and finished with care, even plywood can be made to give your toy a variety of effects. The wings on this biplane were made from common plywood. They were combined with more exotic woods to achieve the contrasting effect.

with the exception of an occasional splinter, you are unlikely to hurt yourself on any piece of wood. Its open network of air-filled cells and fibers makes it a poor conductor of heat, yet wooden objects are never cold to the touch. When treated with care and concern, they yield an unrivaled beauty not found in any other material.

Regardless of region, each variety of tree produces a different structure of cells in its timber. This only becomes visible under the microscope, but this variety of structure results in surface patterns, colors, textures, and lusters that the eye can easily detect and in qualities of weight and hardness that are readily recognizable. Though each pattern is constant for that kind of tree, it can be expressed in different ways in individual trees and even within different parts of the same tree. The method you choose to cut, shape, and finish each wooden toy you make will also give, quite literally, a particular slant on its structure. Due to the variability in all natural materials, no toy illustrated in this book could be reproduced solely for its individual grain feature or specific markings. No two pieces of wood are exactly alike. This is what makes wood fascinating, especially the more exotic types—patterns and properties peculiar to each piece.

Wood identification and selection can be a bit tricky. No wonder. With the vast array of woods from which we can choose the selection seems to be infinite. Fortunately, the factors that are often critical to wood choice—stress, length, expansion and contraction of fibers, durability under excessive wear and tear, and costs based on availablity—are not so critical in toy-making. The descriptions of woods used in many of the projects in this book will help to eliminate some of the guesswork in the wood choices you'll have to make. For our purposes the differences between African Mahogany and Honduras Mahogany or ash and aspen are slight if not negligible. For the discriminating woodworker, however, these differences will be noted. They may be considered especially important if a variety of woods are chosen that closely resemble one another in grain and color.

Color distinctions and differences between sapwood (the newly grown layer of wood just beneath the bark) and heartwood (the older wood at the center of the tree) are important details to notice when differentiating one wood from another. However, color is not the only means. Rings, pores, grain, hardness, and weight may also help to establish the identity of woods if striking color characteristics are not evident. To assist in your choice of woods consult the list in this section (given alphabetically by wood name) and read over the particular features of each wood. Then check for its availability from your wood source or from one provided at the back of this book under **Sources and Suppliers.** Feel comfortable in selecting your wood based on surface appearances, such as color, texture, etc. In time, as your projects take shape, you will develop a like or dislike for certain woods, but be open to including new and different woods as they become available.

You will find that woods, like so many other raw goods, will have ''dry spells'' or will experience ''runs,'' during which times they will be purchased quickly by woodworking enthusiasts.

Many of the more exotic and rare woods are sold by weight rather than linear feet, owing to their scarcity and exorbitant cost. If you need a small piece of wood for plugs or accents in the toy, this hardly necessitates the buying of a linear foot, which could conceivably be ten times the cost and amount of wood called for at one time. There are wood suppliers who will not sell small pieces by weight, so it is often necessary to call or correspond with someone in charge before contemplating a purchase.

Most kinds of wood are possible to identify by their general appearance. In the technical identification of wood, specific differences can be pointed out. Some woods, such as black walnut, ebony, padouk, and purpleheart, can be identified by their color, which is plainly obvious; others, such as Douglas fir, cypress, and the cedars, can be distinguished by their odor. Also, many woods have a pronounced difference in color between sapwood (from the newer wood layers under the bark) and heartwood (from the core of the tree), whereas in other woods there is no such difference.

The color of wood is not always vivid. In fact, woods with vivid color are in a small minority. Wood color is directly linked to the presence of infiltrated compounds in the cell walls and the concavities of their linings. From ash to ebony, the range is immense and offers to the woodworker enormous selection. Wood charts composed of actual specimens are usually on display at well-stocked lumberyards. If you plan on ordering wood, it is suggested that you consult *What Wood Is That?* by Herbert Edlin, at your local library. It includes actual samples of woods.

If possible, it is always better to go to the source so you can carefully examine the wood before you buy. Knots, pinworm holes, bird pecks, decay in isolated pockets, bird's-eyes, mineral streaks, swirls in grain, and ingrown bark may appear as you work the wood and are usually undesirable if a relatively smooth and uninterrupted project is to result from your finishing efforts. These flaws or irregularities may be desirable from a decorative standpoint, but are objectionable for fine, detailed work.

Although one of the basic themes underlying many of the projects in this book is the use and finishing of the more exotic species of woods, you would do well to consider using scraps or wood from discarded furniture and other objects before investing in new wood. Logs can be secured from tree surgeons, gardeners, the scrap bins in mill yards, and occasionally from the Forestry Service. They will earmark certain felled trees that can be had gratis provided that you do the sawing and hauling. Salvage companies often keep on hand a large variety of wood turnings, laminated beams, and old wood fittings for the person interested in designing objects or features within the home. Search for secondhand furniture that has

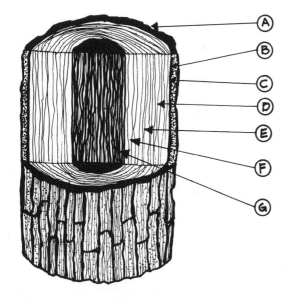

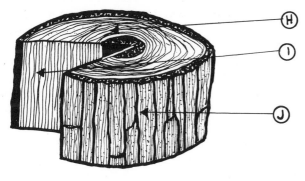

Figure I-4.
Two sections of a tree illustrating its useful parts and the type of cut used to give the wood its unique appearance: A). Outer bark. B). Inner Bark. C). Cambium. D). Pith ray. E). Sapwood. F). Heartwood. G). Pith. H). Transverse cut. I). Radial cut. J). Tangential cut.

Figure I-5.
Striking grain patterns are what characterize different woods. The toy maker would do well to become familiar with all types of wood so that he may wisely select woods to complement his work.

been painted, and, if possible, attempt to identify the wood used in its construction. A small end table might yield a bountiful amount of mahogany, bird's-eye oak, or maple wood and can be had for a few dollars, especially if the piece is somewhat rickety or of dubious value. Solid-core doors, wood window casements, balustrades, railings, and thick counter tops from old hotels, stores, and demolished homes may prove useful and well worth the effort.

Whether you are purchasing new wood or using found scraps, there are certain facts you need to know before you can make intelligent selections. Firstly, there are two general groups of trees—hardwoods and softwoods. The terms "hardwood" and "softwood" refer to the botanical origins of woods and not necessarily to their densities or physical hardnesses. Sap conduction, physical support, and food storage are carried out by cells which constitute a part of the physical makeup of the tree. In general, softwoods have a simpler structure and more consistent overall appearance than hardwoods.

In softwoods, the conduction of sap (a fluid that circulates through the plant, bearing water, food, and essential nutrients) is carried out by thin-walled cells; in hardwoods it is done by vessels. The tree adds a new layer of sap-conducting cells each year, usually in the spring when rapid growth occurs. This layer, a part of each annual ring, is called "springwood."

The physical support in softwoods is made possible by thick-walled cells; in hardwoods it is by fibers. Softwood cells tend to be longer than hardwood fibers. After the spring wood growth, the tree produces a layer of cells or fibers for support called "latewood" or "summerwood." Latewood appears on the outer edge of each annual ring and is often darker or denser than the springwood. In some varieties of hardwoods the spring and summer woods are not distinctly separated. This quality is called "diffuse porous." In "ring-porous" hardwood the springwood is concentrated in a visible band of large pores.

As a general rule, softwoods are softer and easier to work than hardwoods, which are harder and stronger. But there are exceptions in both groups. For example, yellow pine, a softwood, is harder than Philippine mahogany, a hardwood. Softwoods come from cone-bearing trees that often have evergreen needlelike leaves. Hardwoods come from broad-leaved trees, either evergreen or deciduous (those which shed leaves annually).

In both hardwoods and softwoods, storage of food occurs in small boxlike cells arranged in horizontal bands (called "rays"), which run from the center of the tree outward at right angles to the annual rings. Where the rays are large, as in oak and beech, they give a characteristic "figure" on cut surfaces that can be considered beforehand by the woodworker in determining how the wood is to be cut and, eventually, finished. Hardwoods have more obvious rays than softwoods where rays are often indistinguishable to the naked eye.

Terms used in the description of wood are often applied rather loosely. "Grain," for example, can refer to the size of the pores or the direction of the fibers ("straight," "curly," etc.). For the purposes of this book, we will use the following definitions: "Grain" of the wood indicates the direction and nature of the fibers. These can be straight and consistent, or irregular with curves or distortions. Generally, woods with straight grain are easier to handle, but irregular grain can add interest and individuality to the finished piece. "Texture" refers to the overall surface of the wood. If it has large pores or holes, it is "coarse" and if the pores are small, it is "fine." Uniform texture means that the surface is fairly even with pores being similar in size and evenly distributed. "Stability" pertains to the wood's ability to remain the same size and shape once it has been properly dried. A wood which is not stable will absorb moisture in humid conditions and swell. "Durability" refers to the chemical composition of the wood and its ability to resist rot and fungi. Durable woods can be used outdoors without treating them with preservatives. Durability is not critical for toys or other projects that will be used indoors.

The selection of woods is a difficult one, especially when there is a vast array of woods before you from which you are to select the few that are to harmoniously blend and enhance the toy and complement the other woods. Some woods, notably pine, fir, and white cedar, exhibit something less than their more exotic counterparts, ebony, zebrawood, teak, lignum vitae, and tulipwood. However, these should not be overlooked because of their plain appearance, but used for their simple and unaffected features. Many fine utensils, vessels, and objects of universal use, venerated by craftsmen and laymen alike, are made from the more available woods for the very reasons that they are within reach and do the job well. Bamboo, the most universal of all woods, is used in the making of tools, fences, bowls, houses, boats, and even scaffolding more than any other wood of the world. It possesses a low profile when compared to rare wood, which has many of the visual qualities that bamboo lacks. However, for many countries, bamboo works admirably and, in many ways, has no counterpart.

The following woods and their characteristics are provided to assist you in your selection for any of the projects described in the book. Each wood will differ not only in the above-mentioned features, but also in the manner in which it will respond to your tools. Keep a journal of woods, noting their features and workability. This can be a valuable aid for all woodworkers.

If woodworking is new to you, you might begin by selecting woods of contrasting colors or grain markings—zebrawood and ash, padouk and walnut, or a triple laminate of mahogany, beech, and brazilwood.

Hardwoods

Hardwood is the name given to the timber of all broad-leaved trees (as opposed to needled trees which yield softwoods). Hardwoods are usually harder and denser than softwoods, but there are some exceptions. The following is a list of representative hardwoods and their characteristics.

ALDER

Alder wood is white to pale pink or brown when first cut, but turns bright orange-brown with exposure. It has a fine texture with no distinctive figure and is relatively light in weight for a hardwood. It has moderate density and strength, but is not very durable (will not hold up to outdoor use) and has low shock resistance.

Alder dries easily with some shrinkage, especially in the black and grey European varieties. Red alder, the American species, has low shrinkage. The wood saws easily and one can achieve a good finish provided that tools are kept very sharp. It rotary peels, producing good veneer. Alder veneers (very thin sheets) are obtained by rotary peeling. The log is turned on a large lathe and thin sheets are peeled from the circumference by a very sharp blade.

Alder can can be found widely in the Northern Hemisphere and the tree usually grows to modest height on wet sites. It is used for furniture and small items, such as handles and toys.

APPLE

Though generally more important for its fruit than its timber, the apple provides a very fine-textured wood suitable for a number of special uses. The grain is often distorted or spiraled because the trees tend to grow irregularly. Both wild and cultivated varieties produce similar timbers that are a very pale pinkish brown in color.

Apple is a slow-drying wood and will warp or split on occasion. Once seasoned successfully, however, it is stable in use. Hard, strong, and noted for its toughness, apple saws well, but is very hard to split and hard to work, especially where the grain is irregular. It can be machined to a good finish and is receptive to stains and polishes. It turns exceptionally well and can be carved to fine detail.

Some special commercial uses are shuttles, golf club heads, and wooden screws. It is attractive as inlay and is considered a "craft" wood because it is available only in small pieces.

ASH

Ash, which is common to northern climates in various parts of the world, has long been considered an important wood. The tree often reaches remarkable size and was referred to in ancient Norse mythology as "the tree which held up the heavens."

The timber has a pinkish cast when first cut, but pales to nearly white on exposure. The wood is distinctively ring-porous in nature, which means its conspicuous growth rings are marked by large, open pores necessary for rapid spring growth. These well-marked rings appear as lines on radial-cut surfaces (those cut lengthwise from the center of the log) and broad, irregular bands on slash-grain surfaces (also cut lengthwise but farther from the center of the log).

Ash dries readily and is moderately stable, or not likely to shrink, swell, or change shape once dry. If treated, it is suitable for outdoor use. It is a strong wood, noticeably tough and shock resistant. It works well, turns easily, and is especially good for steam bending, a process whereby wood is steamed until it becomes flexible, then bent to the desired curve or shape and allowed to dry. The weight of the wood can vary among species and according to growth speed.

Ash is used where toughness is of the utmost importance in such goods as tennis rackets, hockey sticks, baseball bats, and in other sports equipment. Garden and construction tools often have handles of ash for the same reason, and furniture is another common usage.

BALSA

Balsa, which comes from a fast-growing tropical American tree, is the lightest wood in general use. The best timber is white or slightly pink in color. It is straight grained with a high natural luster and it is distinctly soft and velvety to the touch. Balsa has moderately coarse, but even, texture.

Balsa is easy to dry and is stable after seasoning. It is not strong, but is firm, very easy to work, and can be finished nicely provided that tools are kept very sharp. It is known not only for its lightness, but its unique properties of low thermal conductivity and high sound absorption, as well. These qualities make it ideal for insulating, soundproofing, and for articles requiring great buoyance. In fact, the *Kon Tiki* raft was made of balsa logs and balsa is common in lifesaving equipment.

Perhaps the most commonly known usages for balsa are in model building and theater prop construction. Its light weight and easy workability make it a natural choice for these purposes.

BEECH

Found in tall, thick stands in northern climates, beech rivals oak in popularity among hardwoods. Beech wood is naturally pale brown in color with little variation between the sapwood and heartwood. It is sometimes steamed to lighten the color to pinkish. Beech has a prominent ray figure (the rays being the lines running outward from the center of the log like spokes of a wheel). On surfaces that have been flat or rotary cut the ray markings look like little bands or plates of a darker color. When quarter cut, the rays appear as small dark-brown flecks, evenly scattered over the lighter background.

Beech is of medium weight and is straight grained. It has a fine, even texture, is strong, and quite shock resistant. Beech dries readily, but shrinkage is considered high, and there are occasional problems with distortion. Beech is not terribly stable and is susceptible to humidity changes.

Beech is one of the relatively few woods that can be steam bent; thus it is well known for its use in "bentwood" furniture, where it is steamed and then formed into graceful curves. Beech also turns especially well and can be rotary peeled for veneer. If treated properly, it is acceptable for outdoor use and is used extensively for furniture and tool handles. It is also used for toys and other domestic purposes and makes good flooring.

BIRCH

Birch grows in northern regions and is a lovely white-barked tree with a straight, cylindrical stem and slender branches. Birch wood is pale in color, varying from white to light brownish yellow. Its grain is generally straight, but some varieties (such as flame birch and masur birch) have distinctly figured grains. Its fine, uniform texture makes it the most featureless of all northern hardwoods. It is quite heavy, hard, and dense, and is, therefore, strong and resistant to shock.

In spite of its hardness, birch works well by machine or hand, turns well, and rotary peels for veneer. It shrinks considerably upon drying, but is stable in use. Birch is used for plywood and furniture, and its pulp is important in the production of writing papers. The bark of the tree is noteworthy for its wax content, which makes it waterproof, thus explaining the use of birch in canoe making.

BLACKWOOD (AFRICAN)

Like tulipwood, African blackwood is a distinct species of rosewood that deserves special mention. Its wood is dark brown to black in color, and it has a fine, even texture and grain that may be straight, but is often irregular, since the tree is small and tends to be misshapen.

African blackwood is extremely heavy (almost as heavy as lignum vitae) and has an oily feel. Though it must be dried with great care, it is then stable. The wood can be brittle, is very hard to saw, and must be worked with great care. African blackwood can be turned and bored and is a preferred stock for woodwind instruments.

BOXWOOD

Boxwood has a distinct yellow color and the finest of textures. Its grain is often irregular and it is a very heavy wood. Even when dry, it will barely float in water. Because the tree is small, often only shrub size, timber is usually available in small pieces only.

Boxwood must be dried very carefully to avoid splitting. Once dry, its hardness makes it an excellent wood for turning or carving. Great detail can be achieved because of the very fine texture of this wood, and, therefore, it is often used for engraving. The Bible and other ancient literary works provide us with many historical references to boxwood in small carved pieces, such as combs, toys, and decorative inlay.

BRAZILWOOD

Brazilwood is orange when freshly cut and later deepens to dark red. It is a fine, uniformly textured wood with consistently straight grain. Though characteristically hard and heavy, it works fairly easily and can be finished to a smooth surface.

It was originally harvested as a dyewood (wood from which coloring matter is extracted for dyeing), and the term "brazil" was used in the Middle Ages to identify plants that yielded red dye. When explorers found this small tree in South America, they named the land after the tree.

Brazilwood is not widely used today, but has one special function—the making of violin bows. It provides the right combination of flexibility, strength, and weight for this purpose. Brazilwood can also be found occasionally as decorative inlay.

CEDAR

Although cedar (cedrus) is actually a softwood, the name cedar is often applied to hardwoods that have a similar scent. One such commonly used hardwood with this characteristic is cigar-box cedar or cedrela odorata (also known as "cedro").

The timber of hardwood cedar is the color of mahogany, but has a coarser texture, is lighter weight, and is more resinous. It dries readily and is very stable in use. Though it has good strength for its weight, it could not be considered a strong wood. Very durable and decay resistant, hardwood cedar is used in Central and South America (where it grows) for general construction and furniture. It works easily and well; its uses are limited mostly by its small supply.

A traditional wood for cigar boxes, hardwood cedar is also often used in the building of racing boats.

CHERRY

Cherry, both European and American black, is a fine-textured wood with generally straight grain. It is pale pinkish brown when first cut, but the color darkens to deep red with a characteristic golden sheen sometimes touched with green. Often marked with thin dark-brown bands, streaks, or flecks, it is a particularly lovely and warm wood with a natural glow. When freshly worked cherry has a sweet, roselike scent.

European cherry tends to be marginally heavier than American black cherry, but both are considered to be moderately heavy, strong, and stiff with good shock resistance. Cherry will sometimes distort on drying, but is stable in use. It works well, saws easily, and takes an excellent finish by hand or machine. It is very seldom used outdoors.

Cherry is a well-known wood for furniture and decorative veneers.

CHESTNUT

The large chestnut tree, common in Europe, is known for its fruit and is sometimes recognizable by its spirally fissured bark. Nearly all standing chestnut trees in the United States today are dead, killed by blight. But, because of the durability of the wood, these trees remain a good source of timber.

Chestnut wood is pale brown to greyish and darkens on exposure. It has prominent growth rings like oak, but lacks the silver grain feature of oak. The wood has a coarse texture with growth rings marked by rows of large pores. Relatively light, and low in strength and resistance to shock, chestnut is moderately hard and dries slowly. It is stable in use, however, and is easy to work with hand or machine tools.

Chestnut is naturally durable, especially the heartwood. Its chemical nature, which resists fungi and rot, is such that it may even corrode iron in damp conditions. The wood is often used for fencing and other exterior purposes where great strength is not required. It is rarely used in furniture, but paneling is sometimes made from chestnut veneer.

COCOBOLO

Cocobolo is one of the Central American rosewoods, but its coloration is distinctive enough to give it a singular reputation. When first cut, the wood has almost a rainbow appearance. On exposure the color mellows to a deep orange-red with darker stripes or mottles. It has medium texture and the grain can be straight or irregular. The wood is heavy and very stable once dry.

Cocobolo is not particularly difficult to work considering its weight and hardness. It is an excellent turning wood and though making it difficult to glue successfully, its natural oil contributes to a beautiful finish. It is used for a variety of decorative purposes. A particularly important usage is in knife handles; the natural oils allow for repeated washings without deterioration.

Special care should be taken when working with cocobolo, as its dust can be very irritating and can stain the skin.

EBONY

Though ebony is quite a rare wood, it is familiar because of its traditional use in piano keys. The intense black-colored type is the most well-known, but species vary from the warm black to medium or dark brown Macassar ebony (which has black stripes), to the grey-brown mottled wood of coromandel, and to the very pale white ebonies, such as persimmon.

Ebony has a fine, even texture and is extremely heavy. It must be handled with care and skill in both seasoning and working. It tends to be brittle and is very hard. Ebony can be machined to an excellent finish and has its own natural luster. It is popular for small turned items and has been used as a precious wood for centuries, as indicated by its presence in ancient Egyptian tombs.

ELM

A prominent ring-growth figure and coarse texture are earmarks of elm. With the exception of wych elm, which has a greenish cast, elm is generally pale brown to reddish in color. Elm has a definitive pattern of large and small vessels visible in the irregular grain, which give it a feathery look often referred to as "partridge-breast" figure.

Strength properties and weight vary somewhat among the species. Rock elm is pale and heavy and quite strong, wych elm is dense and moderately hard and stiff; others are moderately light in weight and not notably strong. Elm dries readily, though with some distortion due to the grain irregularities. This irregular grain makes elm almost impossible to split, and it is used in furniture, particularly Windsor chair seats, because of this feature. Elm works well, turns satisfactorily, and bends well.

The timber is not particularly durable, but it survives well in a waterlogged state. Therefore, prime uses are in fishing boat construction, coffins, and even historically as drain pipes. Bored pieces that were used for this purpose hundreds of years ago have been recovered in excellent condition.

HICKORY

Hickory is an American wood found in the eastern half of the United States and Canada. True hickory includes the wood of four species. Other hickory species produce pecan hickory, which is similar but generally inferior in most respects to true hickory.

Hickory has thick white sapwood and red-brown heartwood. The texture is coarse due to its ring-porous nature (the growth rings being marked by rows of large pores). It is generally straight grained and is dense, stiff, hard, and heavy, with the unique ability to withstand sudden pressure. It dries slowly with high shrinkage and is rather difficult to work. The white wood is generally preferable; irregularly grained and knotty pieces are to be avoided.

Hickory is chosen where strength and toughness are prime considerations. Such things as tool handles and athletic goods are often made of hickory. An interesting usage of hickory is in the smoking of food, where it imparts a distinct odor while slowly burning.

HOLLY

The glossy, spiked leaves and red berries of the holly have made it most familiar to us as a Christmas decoration. Though not in great commercial demand, the wood is sometimes available in small pieces.

Holly wood is white to grey-white in color and quite plain in appearance. It has a fine, even texture and often irregular grain. Heavy and hard, it is best dried in small pieces to prevent distortion and holly is not very stable in damp environments.

Though quite difficult to work, holly can be machined to a smooth surface and stains very well. It is generally seen in small turned items and is used for engraving. Holly is often dyed black and used as a substitute for ebony.

HORSE CHESTNUT

Known in America as "the buckeye," horse chestnut is a creamy-white wood (similar to poplar) that is light in weight and has a fine texture. It is a rather plain wood, usually having a straight grain, though older trees sometimes produce irregularly grained timber.

The wood works easily, and dries well with only moderate shrinkage. Once dry, it is stable, but tends to be weak, brittle, and soft. Sharp tools are required to obtain a good finish, and the wood must be treated for outdoor use. It can be sawed and turned and is used commercially for a variety of general purposes.

LIGNUM VITAE

Lignum vitae is the heaviest wood in commercial use. It has a distinctive greenish black color, is highly resinous, and has a very fine texture and closely interlocked grain. It is very strong and hard with excellent resistance to abrasion.

The resin from this small South American tree was once thought to be curative; thus it was given its name, *lignum vitae*, or "wood of life." Though no longer considered medicinal, the resin does impart to the wood the quality of self-lubrication. Though difficult to dry and to work, it is excellent for turning and can be brought to a very fine finish.

Because of the density, durability, and hardness of the wood, it has a unique commercial use in the bearing surfaces of ship propeller shafts where it wears very slowly and produces its own lubrication. Historically, flat-green and crown-green bowls were made of lignum vitae. Today, however, the unavailability of the wood in even moderately sized pieces has limited its use considerably.

LIME

Lime wood is also known as "basswood" and "linden" and is a pale yellow, almost white, wood. There is no distinction between heart and sapwood and both darken to light brown on exposure. It is a straight-grained timber with a fine, uniform texture, is featureless, and has no odor or taste. Light in weight and rather soft, lime wood has a natural luster.

Lime dries quickly and well with some distortion and high shrinkage. It has good stability, but no resistance to decay. Though not a strong wood, it has good working properties, including turning and bending. It is soft enough to be carved with ease, but firm enough for detailed work, and it takes stain readily.

The works of Grinling Gibbons and other master wood-carvers attest to the fact that lime is a favored wood for carving. It is also used for piano parts and small turned items.

MAGNOLIA

Only three species of magnolia are used commercially to any extent. These medium- to large-sized trees are commonly known as "cucumber tree," "Southern magnolia," and "sweet bay." Over sixty other species, many of which are much smaller in size, are generally cultivated for their flowers in the Americas and East Asia.

Magnolia is a pale wood—the sapwood being white to pale yellow sometimes with a greenish cast, the heartwood being pale brown. It has very fine, even texture and straight grain. This plain, featureless wood works well and is moderately hard and stiff. It dries satisfactorily with moderate shrinkage and has good shock resistance. It nails without splitting, turns well, and finishes very nicely. Not resistant to decay, it must be treated for outdoor use. Magnolia is low in compression and bending strengths.

Used commercially for a variety of general purposes, such as packaging, framing furniture, and venetian blinds, magnolia can also be sliced for veneer.

MAHOGANY (AFRICAN)

Closely related botanically to American mahogany, African mahogany was first harvested to augment supplies of true mahogany from South America. Now African mahogany is accepted worldwide as mahogany. Mahogany is a pale pink to reddish brown wood of medium texture with interlocked grain. Its characteristic striped figure is generally less pronounced than in American mahogany, and, on close examination, the pores can be seen in small clusters. It is relatively light in weight and easy to dry. Although stable in use, African mahogany is not quite as consistent as American varieties. African mahogany is moderate in durability and strength and can be somewhat brittle. It works well and finishes well, but special care is required with quarter-cut surfaces.

The popularity of mahogany as a furniture wood varies. Though once very fashionable, except in reproductions it is used much less today. Its use as a general purpose wood for joinery, desks, doors, and decorative veneer continues to keep the demand for it substantial.

MAHOGANY

The original mahogany was the Cuban variety, a heavy, deep red-brown wood that is rare today. The most frequently used species today are the Central Americans, along with five African woods that are very similar (see **Mahogany African**). The color of American mahogany is a bit lighter than Cuban mahogany, and the wood is of medium texture. The wood sometimes appears featureless, but may have a striped pattern and is occasionally highly figured. American wood can be distinguished from African by the arrangement of its pores. In American species the pores are evenly spread through the wood; in the African varieties they are found grouped in small clusters.

Mahogany is easy to dry and very stable in use. It saws easily and can be machined to an excellent finish. Late eighteenth-century furniture designers, such as Chippendale and Hepplewhite, gave mahogany its reputation as a fine furniture wood.

MAPLE

There are a number of species of maple and they are generally classified into two groups, hard and soft. Sugar and black maples are known as hard and are correspondingly heavier and somewhat stronger than soft maples, such as silver, red, and box elder. The best known of the maples is the sugar maple, famous for its sweet sap, which is converted into syrup. All maples are known and loved for their brilliantly colored autumn leaves.

Maple woods are all similar in their pale red-brown color. The heartwood tends to be a bit darker and is heavy, strong, stiff, and hard. The soft maples are about twenty-five percent lighter in weight than the hard. Shock resistance is good, but none are durable in weathering conditions. Maple is usually straight grained, but sugar maples occasionally produce "bird's-eye" figures, where the starting points of new side branches appear as small brown spots with dark centers looking rather like eyes. These contrast with the pale background of the wood, creating a distinctly lovely pattern. When these logs are discovered, they are almost always rotary peeled for veneer, the only process by which the grain is fully displayed.

Maple dries fairly well, but with high shrinkage. When seasoned, it is very stable and has fine working properties. It is a favorite of carvers and turners, works to a smooth finish, and wears slowly. Maple is used extensively for furniture, flooring, veneer, shoemakers' lasts, and a variety of wooden ware.

OAK (RED)

Red oak is distinguished from white oak by the color of its heartwood which is more pinkish. It is used less for commercial purposes and is generally considered inferior to white oak. The coarse texture is similar and red oaks have the same silver grain figure on quarter-cut surfaces, but the rays are shorter and the figure not so well marked.

Red oak is less durable than white and must be treated for outdoor use. It is a very dense wood, is difficult to dry, and is also more difficult to work than white oak. Suitable for interior work, red oak has many of the same uses as white oak, though the latter is usually preferred.

OAK (WHITE)

White oak includes several species of European, Japanese, and American trees with similar timber. The sapwood of white oak is nearly white and the heartwood is pale yellowish brown, sometimes greyish. White oak is typically coarse textured and ring porous in nature, the pores being filled with tiny hairlike structures that make the wood quite waterproof.

The grain of oak is usually straight with obvious growth rings and rays. When quarter sawn (cut from the center to the outside edge), oak has a distinctive "silver grain" figure. This silver grain reveals the rays as broad bands that are harder and smoother than the surrounding wood and that reflect light quite noticeably, giving it a silvery sheen. Wood used in furniture is often quarter sawn to take advantage of this unique property.

White oak is moderately heavy, dense, strong, and tough. It is relatively difficult to work owing to its weight and density. It is naturally durable due to the tannins (chemical compounds which are natural preservatives) in the wood, which give it the odor of tannic acid when worked. The tannins will react with iron causing "ink stains," so wooden pegs are often used to join oak, which is, in any case, difficult to nail.

Oak is a favorite furniture wood and is used for flooring, construction, and for whiskey and sherry casks. It is a preferred wood wherever strength, durability, and appearance count.

PADOUK

Padouk is the name for a group of exotic woods that are known for their striking color. African padouk heartwood is purple-red to purple-brown, while that of Andaman padouk is crimson with darker markings. These are coarse-textured woods with interlocked grains. They are heavy, very strong and solid, and are noted for their decay resistance.

Padouk dries slowly, but well, and is exceptionally stable when dry. Considering its weight and strength, padouk is not unduly difficult to work and finishes very well. It is a favored wood for boat building and is used in joinery, counters, pool tables, and for tool handles. Its properties of strength and unusual beauty make it understandably popular for a number of purposes.

PEAR

Sometimes known as "fruitwood," pear wood can be distinguished by its exceptionally fine and uniform texture. It is a pale, but rich, pinkish brown and is generally straight grained. Irregular grain is not uncommon, however, from gnarled or misshapen trees.

Pear wood is moderately heavy, is strong, and is known for its toughness. It dries slowly and tends to distort, especially if irregular grain is present, but is very stable once dry. It is hard to split or saw, but machines well and turns extremely well. Pear wood yields a fine finish and

can be used for veneer. It is not naturally decay resistant.

Because its fine texture holds up in the most intricate of work, pear is a favorite among wood-carvers. The wood is in short supply since the tree is generally grown for its fruit and wild pear is not widely available. The timber, therefore, generally comes from old orchard trees. Used for small turned and carved items, inlay, and tableware, pear wood is often used for rulers and drawing instruments because it can be worked to fit precise requirements and will then remain stable.

PERSIMMON

Persimmon wood is a white ebony, and, though similar in some respects to darker ebonies, its color and working properties are significantly different. The sapwood is off-white with a greyish cast. The small core of heartwood may have more color, but is rarely used commercially because of its meager amount. Persimmon is dense with a fine, even texture and usually straight grain.

It dries fairly easily, but is not very stable and may change with humidity variations. Hard and strong, it can be worked to an excellent finish that wears well, and persimmon has good impact resistance. Persimmon can be worked to show intricate and precise detail and is chosen for small industry items, such as spools and shuttles. It is also used for golf club heads because of its smooth finish and impact resistance.

Persimmon is native to the United States and has an edible fruit that is a beautiful pink-orange hue. There are other white ebonies, but none are of commercial value.

POPLAR

Poplar (sometimes called "cottonwood" in North America) includes a large number of species that have similar woods. The aspen is one of the best known of these. Poplar wood is white, often having a pink, grey, or brown tint. It has straight grain and fine, even texture. One of the lightest commercial hardwoods, poplar is rather soft and fibrous and can often be identified by a fuzzy or wooly surface, which is the result of the number of large pores needed for water conduction in the fast-growing season.

Poplar is not a strong wood, but it is considered tough for its weight. It does not split or splinter and it dries well with good stability. It is easy to work and saws well, but is most successfully handled with sharp tools. Poplar is susceptible to decay, so it is generally used for indoor purposes.

Its most well-known use is in match sticks, but poplar veneer is also woven into baskets and used for plywood.

PURPLEHEART

Sometimes called "ameranth," purpleheart is one of the most distinctly colored of all woods. Though a dull brown when the wood is first cut, the color fast becomes bright purple and then, over long exposure, gradually changes to a rich brown-red. Produced by about twenty species of large South American trees, the woods vary in texture from fine to moderately coarse. Figured wood is rare and the grains vary from straight to interlocked with a very occasional wavy look.

Purpleheart is a heavy wood and is very strong, dense, and tough. It dries well, if rather slowly, and is then quite stable. Because of its remarkable density and durability, it is difficult to saw and will dull tools rapidly. Once finished, it wears very slowly.

Despite its unusual color, purpleheart is seldom used as a decorative wood. Instead, it is more in demand for its properties of strength for heavy construction. A common place to find it is in the butt of a billiard cue where both its strength and beauty play a part.

ROSEWOOD

Rosewood is one of the most prized and sought-after timbers because of its unusual color and exotic figuring. The pale sapwood from this small tree is generally discarded; it is the red to purple-brown heartwood with its dark markings that is prized. Figuring and coloration of the wood varies somewhat with species, and, because rosewood trees are generally small, wood is usually only available in short lengths.

Rosewood is hard and very heavy. It dries fairly well, but works with some difficulty. When freshly cut, it often emits a roselike scent. It can be worked to a fine finish and has an almost silvery sparkle (produced by the shiny gum filling in its rather coarse pores) on longitudinal surfaces. It turns well and can be sliced for veneer.

Rosewood has long been favored for fine cabinetry and furniture and is preferred for xylophone keys and marimbas. It is often used in inlay work.

SANDALWOOD

Sandalwood has been coveted since classical times both for its wood and precious oil. True sandalwood comes from India. It is a small tree that is actually a parasite of the roots of other trees, but other species have been discovered that have a similar scent. The scent of sandalwood is, unlike many others, persistent and can be detected long after the wood has been dried and worked.

Sandalwood is pale yellow or brown when first cut, but darkens to a medium brown over time. It has a very fine, even texture and a straight to irregular grain. It is a heavy wood and is naturally durable with an oily feel. It dries very slowly, but does not split and has excellent working properties. Sandalwood carves especially well, and its natural oils contribute to a lustrous finish.

Long used for carving, especially for ornate boxes and combs, sandalwood is also distilled for its oil, which is used in perfumery.

SILKY OAK

Though not a true oak botanically, silky oak is similar in appearance, and, importantly, has the same silver grain (bands of denser wood which have a silvery shine) when quarter sawn. It is pinkish brown in color with a coarse texture resembling that of oak, but it is about one-third lighter. Originating from a large Australian tree, the wood must be dried carefully, but then works well and has some advantages over true oak in workability because of its lighter weight.

Silky oak can be sawed and nailed without splitting. It holds well and can be worked to a good finish. Though tough and strong for its weight, it cannot be compared to true oak for these qualities. It can, however, be steam bent and peeled for veneer.

Because of its silver grain, the wood is used for decorative effects in furniture and paneling, especially in its native land. Outside of Australia it is mainly used in veneer form

SYCAMORE

This species of maple is also known as "buttonball" and "buttonwood," but sycamore is its most familiar name. Its wood is reddish brown, sometimes with a greyish tinge, and it is often stained grey in commercial use. Somewhat softer than other maples, sycamore has a fine texture and interlocked grain. It has been characterized as moderate in hardness, strength, and stiffness and has good shock resistance. It is moderately heavy and shrinks somewhat in drying.

Because it is softer than other maples, sycamore is preferable for carving. Certain trees produce very attractive irregular grain and, when found, command a high price. One unique use for the figured wood, with its ripples or dapples of light and dark, is in violin parts, especially the backs; thus, the term "fiddle back" figure has come to be the name applied to this special quality of sycamore. Other uses include a variety of general products, such as lumber, veneer, flooring, and butcher blocks.

TEAK

True teak (tectona grandis) is native to Burma and Thailand and is one of the world's great woods. The coloration is usually a uniform golden brown, sometimes with a hint of green, but the wood may be darker brown and may have very dark markings. It has a coarse texture, which can be quite irregular, and a dull surface with no natural luster. It is ring porous and has a definite growth-ring figure appearing on flat-sawn surfaces.

Teak is a heavy wood. Before drying, it will sink in water. It has a leathery smell, an oily feel, and is high in natural durability. Teak dries slowly, but well, and is known for its stability. It is very strong for its weight and hard to saw or work by machine because it is abrasive in nature. It is so difficult to nail that is is usually bored first.

Teak's combination of strength, stability, and durability make it obviously long wearing. It is used for shipbuilding and is preferred above all other woods for decking. Other uses include construction and furniture. Because of its ability to resist acids, it is used for laboratory finishings.

TULIPWOOD

Tulipwood is botanically related to rosewood, but varies significantly in appearance from other species. Its wood is creamy yellow and the figure markings are pink to reddish purple stripes. The colors fade somewhat on exposure, but remain distinctive. The grain of tulipwood is straight or interlocked and it has a very fine texture.

Because of its considerable weight, tulipwood is sometimes difficult to dry and tends to split. Like other rosewoods, it is very hard and, therefore, difficult to machine, but it will take a high polish. It has the characteristic rose fragrance when freshly cut. Tulipwood slices successfully for veneer and, therefore, is used in various ornamental ways.

WALNUT

The name walnut is sometimes applied rather loosely to a variety of brown figured woods, but only the genus *juglans* is true walnut. European species produce timber that is grey-brown, often with a pinkish tinge, with black streaks. Often highly figured with wavy dark bands, walnut is a most beautiful wood chosen for its decorativeness.

The grain is straight to wavy and the wood is of medium texture. It is hard, strong, heavy, and has good natural durability. These properties of strength make it obviously desirable for any number of uses. It dries slowly, but is then quite stable. It works quite easily and finishes especially well to a smooth, lustrous surface. Veneer is used for paneling and the wood has long been used in fine furniture (excellent examples can be found in furniture of the Queen Anne period). It is preferred wood for gun stocks because of its appearance, stability, and shock resistance.

The American black walnut (*J. nigra*) is unique among the walnuts for its more uniform purple- to chocolate-brown coloration. It has a coarser texture and a distinctive odor and even taste. It is often chosen for its rich color and has much the same working properties as other walnuts.

WILLOW (BLACK)

The Mississippi valley is the origin of the black willow, most important among the willows for commercial purposes. The wood is much like poplar—generally featureless with fine, even texture. Black willow may be greyish or reddish brown with darker streaks.

Though shrinkage is substantial, the wood dries quickly and consistently. It is stable in use. Black willow is a low-strength wood, rather soft, but resistant to shock and especially to splintering. It works easily and finishes well.

Because it is lightweight and yet tough, willow is used for artificial limbs. It is considered the best wood for cricket bats because it can absorb blows without splintering, and it makes satisfactory flooring.

ZEBRAWOOD

Zebrawood comes from two species of large African trees. The pale sapwood is generally discarded and the highly decorative heartwood alone is marketed. It is straw-colored to pale brown with abundant dark brown to black stripes. When quarter-sawn, these appear as parallel lines, and, on flat- or rotary-cut surfaces, they produce an irregular wavy pattern.

Zebrawood is a coarse-textured, moderately dense wood with interlocked grain. It is heavier than oak, with good strength and shock resistance. It is hard to dry because of a tendency to twist, and, for this reason, quarter-sawn pieces are the most reliable. The wood takes a good finish by hand or machine, saws readily, and slices or peels well for veneer. It is decay resistant.

Generally seen as veneer, zebrawood is used for a variety of decorative purposes, often as inlay in furniture and cabinetry. It is also used for small turned items and makes very exotic paneling.

Softwoods

Softwoods come from coniferous (cone-bearing) trees or those with needlelike leaves. They are generally softer and easier to work than hardwoods and have a simpler structure (and, therefore, less pattern or figure). Only softwoods may have resin, which gives them a turpentine odor, expecially when freshly cut. The following list covers most common softwoods.

CEDAR

A true softwood, cedar comes from four species of large evergreens that are found only in high mountainous regions with peculiar climates. One of these, the cedar of Lebanon, is historically important and was used in the royal tombs of ancient Egypt.

The wood is a pale, warm brown with obvious growth rings that are unusual in their irregular, wavy appearance. (In most other woods growth rings form regular, smooth circles.) Cedar is often identified by its fragrance, which is somewhat like incense. It is of medium weight and dries well with some distortion. It is brittle and not particularly strong, but is noted for its resistance to fungi and termites. It is very durable, having been known to last for centuries. Cedar works easily and takes a fine finish.

Used locally for construction and fences, the wood is found internationally in furniture and as decorative sliced veneer. Cedar closets and chests have long been used for storage of clothing and linens.

CEDAR (YELLOW)

The wood of yellow cedar is pale yellow and has a strong cedarlike smell when first cut. It is native to the Pacific coast of North America and is actually not a true cedar. Its very slow growth provides a fine, even texture and it is straight grained.

Yellow cedar dries well with little shrinkage. Its fragrance dissipates in the drying process, leaving only a faint potatolike smell. Once dry, it is noted for its stability and durability. It is moderately strong, stiff for its weight, and has good shock resistance. It works easily and well and provides a good finish. Yellow cedar is an attractive and versatile wood, and is, unfortunately, quite rare. It is excellent for outdoor uses because of its durability and is used for surveyors' poles and engineering patterns because of its added stability.

CYPRESS

True cypress demands a warm climate, but is not naturally prolific anywhere. The tree grows very rapidly and it has been planted successfully, but still does not have much commercial value because it tends to be knotty and, therefore, hard to work. The coloration in true cypress is pale yellow to brown, and it is generally straight grained with fine texture. It is light, nonresinous, and has a faint cedarlike smell.

Cypress dries quickly and well. It is moderately strong and durable, works easily, and can be finished nicely, but the knots and irregular grain around them can be difficult to handle.

Sawed wood is used for general construction and outdoor uses. Selected pieces are used for interior work.

DOUGLAS FIR

This outstanding softwood comes from a magnificent tree native to the northern Pacific coast of the United States and Canada. Douglas fir rivals the sequoia in height, and trees have been found over one thousand years in age. The tree can be identified by its unique bark, which has a cinnamon-red coloration in the cracks, or fissures.

The wood is pale to medium red-brown, turning yellowish in old trees. It has a conspicuous growth-ring figure, particularly evident on flat-sawn and rotary-cut surfaces. The wood is usually straight grained and often is rather resinous. Weight varies considerably, but is generally medium. The wood dries quickly and well. Douglas fir is considered strong and firm, works well by hand or machine, and has a tendency to splinter, which can be reduced by quarter sawing.

Douglas fir is the leading structural wood of North America. Very large sizes are available, making it the most important source of plywood. The attractive flaming grain is an asset to interior carpentry and it has been used in furniture, though not frequently.

FIR

The true firs are species of Abies. Though botanically incorrect, the name is sometimes applied to other woods, notably the Douglas fir. There are many species that produce similar timber, and there is no distinction made between the heart and sapwoods, which range from creamy white to pale brown. The firs are nonresinous and odorless, with little or no natural luster.

The wood is light in weight, typically straight grained, and dries easily and well. It is low in strength and tends to be brittle, soft, and hard to preserve, but it is easy to work and can be finished nicely with sharp tools.

Fir is an important pulpwood in North America and is used internationally for building, packaging, and joinery.

HEMLOCK

Hemlocks are generally identified as eastern and western and grow in corresponding regions of North America. The western hemlock is a larger tree, and most commercial timber is of this variety, since it is generally of superior quality.

Western hemlock is pale, almost white, in color with streaks of brown or purplish grey caused by the presence of bark maggots. These streaks do not affect the strength of the wood. The frequent small, round black knots are sound and tight. The wood is nonresinous and straight grained with well-marked growth rings. It is of medium weight for a softwood. Eastern hemlock is quite similar, but somewhat coarser and lighter in weight.

The wood dries slowly with large shrinkage. It is moderately stable in use and moderately hard and stiff with average shock resistance. It is not a strong wood and not resistant to decay, but works well and takes a good finish.

Western hemlock is an important commercial timber used for construction and structural purposes. It is also a source of pulp and plywood.

PINE (EASTERN WHITE)

Eastern white pine is a soft pine native to the eastern United States and Canada. Its wood is pale yellow to light brown often with a pink or red cast and it generally darkens on exposure. The grain is straight and the growth rings are not well defined, but the fine, uniform texture is noteworthy.

Known as "yellow pine" in Europe, this soft pine is lightweight and low in strength. It dries quickly and well with low shrinkage and good stability after drying. It is not decay resistant. It works very easily, glues particularly well, and gives an excellent finish.

The demand for quality wood is high. Since it can be cut to fine detail and is very stable, it is often used for engineering patterns. Other uses include paneling, organ parts, toys, rollers, and a variety of other items.

PINE (JACK)

As with many of the pines, this species is known by several common names, including "scrub," "grey," and "black pine." The timber of jack pine has clearly distinguishable white sapwood, which sometimes comprises half the tree. The heartwood is light brown or orange. It is rather coarse in texture, somewhat resinous, and relatively light in weight.

Jack pine is low in many strength categories—bending, compression, stiffness, and shock resistance. It is often knotty, but dries well with little shrinkage. Principally it is used for pulpwood, fuel, and packaging.

PINE (PITCH)

Pitch pine is the heaviest softwood used commercially. It includes several species that produce some of the heaviest and strongest pine timber. Pitch pine is highly resinous. Its yellow sapwood is easily distinguished from the red-brown heartwood and growth rings are very evident, each clearly marked by a band of darker, dense latewood or summerwood. (Latewood is produced by the tree for structural support after it has added its new layer of springwood.)

Pitch pine dries slowly and will sometimes split. It is moderately hard, strong, and stiff with good shock resistance, and it is fairly durable. Pitch pine is rather hard to work and the resin may be troublesome, as it tends to build up on tools.

Pitch pine is used in industrial construction and is a traditional wood for school desks and church furniture, where its strength and hardness ensure long wear.

PINE (PONDEROSA)

A very large tree, the ponderosa pine grows quickly and has been known to live over seven hundred years. Other common names include "bull pine" and "black jack" (common in western states). Ponderosa is of the yellow pine group, but looks somewhat like the white pines. The heartwood is a light red-brown and the wide sapwood is nearly white, tending to pale yellow. It has straight grain and uniform texture. When knots are present, they are generally in groups with knot-free timber in between, as this is a characteristic branching pattern of pines in general.

Ponderosa will give off a strong turpentinelike smell when first cut, but this fades. It dries well with little shrinkage, is moderately light, quite soft, and is rather low in strength and stiffness. It also has low shock resistance.

Ponderosa pine is one of the most important timbers in the West for general building purposes. It must be treated for outdoor use, but this can be done successfully. Veneers are often rotary cut, revealing a flame pattern with groups of round reddish brown or black knots, and are used for traditional pine paneling.

PINE (RED)

Red pine is also known as "Norway pine" and is sometimes grouped with white pine in commercial sale. The heartwood of red pine is pale red to red-brown and the sapwood is almost white with a yellow tinge. The growth rings are quite distinct and it is straight grained for the most part. The texture is not as even as in Eastern white pine and the wood is somewhat resinous.

Red pine is moderately heavy and moderately soft. It falls in the medium range of strength, stiffness, and shock resistance. It dries fairly well, but shrinks considerably, and, after seasoning, it is stable in use.

Red pine is used in flooring and siding plus a variety of general construction purposes.

PINE (SCOTS)

Often called "redwood," because of the reddish heartwood, Scots pine has a very broad range throughout Europe, Asia, Scandinavia, Russia, Poland, and Japan. The growth rings are generally well marked, but the nature of the wood varies considerably depending on its source. Slow-grown trees (such as the northern Russian stock) produce fine-textured, dense wood.

The timber, in general, is mildly resinous and often knotty. Light in weight compared to most hardwoods, it would be considered of medium weight for a softwood. It is stable in use after seasoning and has good strength for its weight. It works well and finishes nicely, but is not naturally durable.

Scots pine is generally used for house building and, occasionally, for furniture. It is an important pulpwood for wrapping paper.

PINE (SOUTHERN YELLOW)

Four pine species are grouped commercially under the heading of Southern yellow pine. These are longleaf (P. polustris), shortleaf (P. enchata), Loblolly (P. taeda) and slash (P. elliottii). These are among the heaviest and hardest of the pines and thus the preferred timbers for most uses.

The sapwood of the Western yellow pine is a yellowish white, the heartwood, a reddish brown. The growth rings are quite distinct and characterized by a band of dense latewood. The wood is heavy, strong, and stiff. It is hard and moderately high in shock resistance. Shrinkage can be high upon drying, but the resulting timber is stable in use. The wood is not naturally durable and must be preserved for outdoor uses.

Southern yellow pine is most generally used in construction and furniture. Lower-grade timber has a variety of uses in rough carpentry and packaging, where strength requirements are lower.

PINE (SUGAR)

Found along the western coast of the United States, sugar pine is also known as "California pine." Its heartwood is buff-colored to light or reddish brown and the sapwood is creamy. It is straight grained and has a fairly uniform texture.

Sugar pine is easy to work. It saws well and is easy to nail, it dries well with very little shrinkage, and it is quite stable, staying in place well after seasoning. It is a light wood, low in strength, and moderately soft; stiffness and shock resistance are rated low.

Sugar pine is used extensively for lumber because it can be milled in large pieces of very good quality. Since it is so easy to saw and nail, it is a favorite for interior carpentry and can be found throughout an average house wherever great strength is not required.

SEQUOIA

Often called "redwood" for its distinctly reddish color, this timber comes from one of the tallest of all trees and grows only in California. It is closely related to the giant sequoia, which grows to mammoth proportions and is now a protected species.

The reddish brown wood is typically straight grained and nonresinous with a clearly marked growth-ring figure. The wood is lightweight but firm and is moderately strong and stiff. It dries well and is stable in use. Noted for its decay resistance, sequoia works easily and takes an excellent finish, provided it is worked with very sharp tools. It also splits particularly well.

Stable and durable, redwood is used for any number of uses, including fencing and garden furniture. It is excellent for window and door construction and other joinery.

SPRUCE

Second to pine in commercial softwoods, spruce is particularly important in North America, where it abounds in coniferous forests. In Europe, it is known as "whitewood."

Spruce is a wood of high natural luster, almost white in color. Some wood is pinkish, notably that of the Western Sitka spruce. It is straight grained with moderately fine and even texture. It dries fast and consistently and has good strength (this is especially true of Sitka), works easily, finishes well, and is less resinous than the pines. Spruce is not decay resistant.

Spruce is used as a structural wood and for interior joinery. It is important as a pulpwood, especially for newsprint because of its white color. Special uses for selected wood include the fronts of violins and piano soundboards. Veneers are used for core material in various plywoods.

TAMARACK

Tamarack, also known as "larch," is unique among the softwoods because it sheds its leaves in the winter. Tamarack sapwood is whitish and the heartwood is usually yellow-brown to rust-brown. It is a coarse-textured wood with growth rings well defined by the distinct contrast between early and latewood.

Quite dense and heavy, the wood is considered moderate in most strength properties. It is notably tough and somewhat resistant to decay. It may distort in drying, but is stable in use. While not difficult to work, care must be taken where knots are present, especially in the finishing process.

Tamarack is a good choice for outdoor use and is traditional for fishing-boat construction. It is used as an estate wood and for general construction and packaging purposes. In the round it is used as pole and post stock.

YEW

This beautiful wood is very slowly grown and is one of the heaviest of the softwoods. When first cut, the wood is reddish, but it turns brown with long exposure. Growth rings are evident, though not well marked, and the texture is very fine and even. Irregular grain often makes the wood especially decorative.

Yew dries well and fairly rapidly. It is strong and has almost the hardness of oak. The wood is particularly resistant to splitting and is known for its resilience—it is one of the few softwoods that can be steam bent. Yew works well, turns well, and is durable. Care is needed in finishing because of the irregularities in grain, but a smooth surface can be achieved.

A traditional use of yew is in archers' bows, where its strength and suppleness are important. It is also a fine furniture wood, and veneers are used for various decorative purposes.

EQUIPMENT FOR TOY MAKING

Tools for shaping wood are as indispensable to the making of toys as the wood itself. Almost all of the tools we use today have their roots in the past. Stone age hammers had no handles, but were hollowed on one side for a comfortable thumb grip. When primitive man first put a handle on his hammer, he grooved the stone head so a flexible withe could be bent around it and bound. The bit brace of the nineteenth century was often made by the man who used it and then handsomely carved to advertise his skill. Less elaborate models were sold to others.

Today, tools have become highly specialized and, with the continued growth of power tools, woodworking has become a very popular craft for everyone. But new tools require as much skill as the old, established ones. What is different is the kind of skill or skills required. Do not be concerned if your home workshop is not furnished with *all* of the following tools; very few are. Purchase tools as the need arises. Remember too that power tools, although rarely a hindrance, often create a dependence and can take away from the "feel" of handcrafting your works. Before the drill press there was and still remains the hand drill.

*Figure II–1.
A push-pull steel tape measure. Portable and lightweight, it is easily contained in the craftsman's toolbox.*

Hand Tools

The tools are described here for the convenience of the woodworker who wishes to have a little more background on which tools he should use and how to use them for the job at hand. Pick and choose as you go along. Buy tools consistent with affordability. Closely examine the workmanship of each item to safeguard against poor metals and shoddy craftsmanship. Secondhand stores and flea markets often provide good hunting grounds for older, "experienced" tools that should not be overlooked. Tool hunting can be as much fun as toy-making and they certainly complement one another.

RULES
Rules are used to measure and mark wood. Wooden rules, though often less expensive, will wear in time. Metal rules are more durable.

Bench Rule
Bench rules are straight wooden or metal rules made in one piece. They normally have inch or metric gradations. You can test them for straightness by standing them on edge.

Folding Rule
The folding rule is used in a confined space where a long rule would be inconvenient. It also eliminates the inconvenience of carrying a long measuring device around. Those with metal reinforced tips will resist wear.

Push-Pull Steel Tape
This type of rule is an extendable tape device coiled into a metal or plastic container. The spring inside controls an automatic return. It is a very portable type of ruler and won't take up much room in the tool chest.

SQUARES AND BEVELS

Squares and bevels are used to ensure accuracy of angles in woodworking situations where care must be taken.

Framing Square

The framing square is used for calculating, to mark out work for squaring, and to check angles used in wood construction.

Try Square

This is used to mark a line at right angles to an edge and to check that the corners of a frame or joint are accurate. The tool forms an accurate ninety-degree angle both on the inside and outside edges.

Combination Square

This is a steel rule securely clamped in a steel head used for multiple purposes. Some combination squares have a level vial inside the head to measure angulation.

T Square

This is a long ruler, the head of which is fastened at the center to a piece of wood or metal. In effect, it can be used to slide along the edge of the stock and provide a straight edge for marking.

Spring Dividers

The divider is used to scribe arcs or circles on wood or to mark off divisions on a line, and normally has two identical legs with hardened points. They are adjusted by means of a set screw on a threaded shaft. The tool is rotated by turning the knurled spigot on the top.

PUNCHES AND AWLS

Punches and awls are used to pierce and penetrate work, for making identification marks, nailing and drilling, and for driving nails and brads below the wood surface.

Punches

A punch is used to start a hole intended for drilling or to free a metal pin. Lightly tap the punch over the mark using a hammer. This will result in a slight conical depression in the wood. A sheet metal punch can be used to set a nail beneath the surface of the wood. This is to be filled with wood putty afterwards to conceal the nail head.

Awl

A straight-barreled awl is very useful for producing holes in leather or piercing thin veneers of wood. Thicker pieces of wood can have holes started with a brad awl, which is a screwdriver-type awl. This awl prevents the wood from splitting along the axis of the grain.

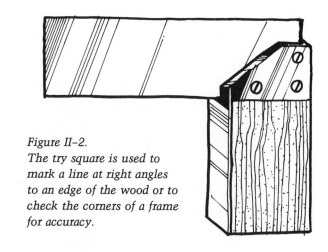

Figure II-2.
The try square is used to mark a line at right angles to an edge of the wood or to check the corners of a frame for accuracy.

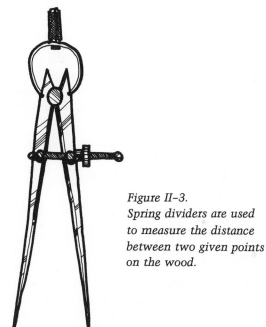

Figure II-3.
Spring dividers are used to measure the distance between two given points on the wood.

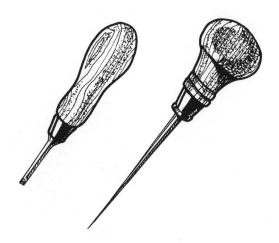

Figure II-4.
On the right is a straight-barreled awl. On the left is a brad awl.

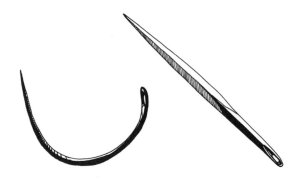

Figure II–5.
Sailcloth needles are used for sewing or mending heavy-duty cloth and leather.

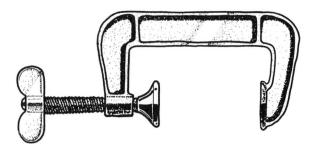

Figure II–6.
An adjustable C-clamp is one of the most versatile clamps available to the woodworker.

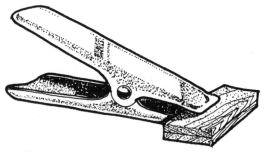

Figure II–7.
Spring clamps are used to provide light pressure when gluing. They can become the woodworker's second pair of hands.

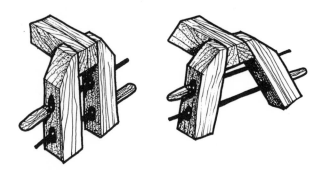

Figure II–8.
Hand screws, sometimes called Jorgensen clamps, adjust to any angle and are especially helpful in clamping wood at odd angles.

Sailcloth Needle

A sailcloth needle is to be used for mending and sewing together coarse and thick fabrics where ordinary needles fail. A hooked needle is useful for getting at awkward places.

CLAMPS

Clamps are devices to be used for holding or pressing work pieces together for gluing, straightening, and other purposes.

C-Clamp

This is a most versatile tool for wood and metal work. Pressure is applied by turning the wing thumbscrew or tommy bar. Use blocks of scrap lumber between the clamp and the work to prevent marking the stock.

Spring Clamps

Spring clamps are manually operated. The jaws are opened by squeezing the handles together. The clamp is then positioned over the work and released. Spring clamps are used to provide light pressure while gluing.

Hand Screw

Sometimes called "parallel clamps," these have been used for hundreds of years and are the real workhorses for clamping any large pieces of wood that will fit within the jaws. Hand screws adjust to any angle and should be used for clamping wood at odd angles. Modern hand screws are fitted with metal spindles in place of a threaded hole in the jaw itself. To adjust the hand screw grip each handle and rotate the tool either toward or away from you to open or close the jaws. Slip the clamp on the work and then tighten accordingly. This is best done by tightening the rear screw. Prevent the clamps from being glued to the wood stock by placing paper between the clamp and the jaw. Better yet, brush melted wax over the parts that will come in contact with the wood.

Pipe Clamp

This tool is used to hold large boards or frames together while gluing. It is fully adjustable, being composed of a long steel bar with a fixed jaw at one end and an adjustable

Figure II–9.
The pipe clamp is used for laminating large and wide pieces of wood edge-to-edge. It is especially valuable in the making of tabletops and other large surface projects.

jaw with a bolt at the other end. The latter is held in place by notches in the bar. Pipe clamps range from 1 foot to 6 feet in length.

HANDSAWS

If a saw is to be useful for cutting wood, the blade must be made of flexible, tempered steel. The teeth are alternately bent to the left or right to make a kerf slightly wider than the blade thickness. This prevents binding. To further prevent binding the blade is made slightly thicker at the back. Several kinds of saws are used by woodworkers; the choice will depend on the job at hand.

Ripsaw

The ripsaw with its chisellike teeth is designed specifically for cutting lumber along its length; that is, with the grain. It has 5, 5½, or 6 large teeth per inch. These have a ripping or chisellike action and do almost all the cutting on the forward stroke. A 26-inch blade length is standard.

Crosscut Saw

This is to be used when cutting across the grain of the wood and for all cutting of plywood. It has small, sharp teeth with knifelike points. Twelve-point saws are called ''panel saws'' and are to be used for very fine work. Blades range from 20 to 28 inches in length.

Backsaw

This is sometimes called a ''tenon saw.'' This tool has a straight blade, parallel top and bottom, and a heavy strip of metal wrapped along the back to provide rigidity. It is used to cut joints and small pieces of wood and for fine detailing. This gives credence to the term ''dovetail saw'' which is widespread in Europe.

Coping Saw

This saw is used to make curved cuts in wood or plastic and for cutting irregular shapes in thin wood or plywood. The blade of the saw is very narrow, has extremely fine teeth, and can be reversed for cutting in either direction. Being removable, the blade is useful for making cuts that must begin with a drilled hole.

Hacksaw

Hacksaws are used to cut most metals. They have a pistol-grip handle with a removable blade. The blade is held under tension by the natural spring of the frame.

Compass Saw

This is used to cut holes in a panel. This saw has no frame, so it can be used in places where a coping saw would be limited by the edge of the board or panel. The blades are 10 to 14 inches long and are available with teeth of several sizes for crosscutting or ripping.

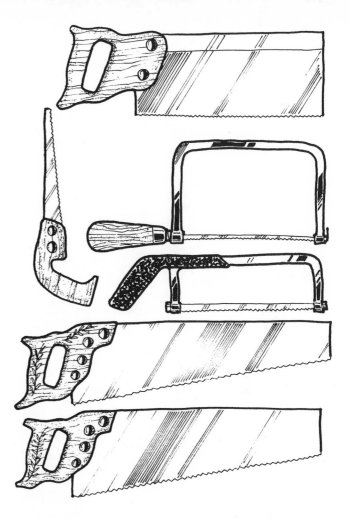

Figure II–10.
A variety of handsaws used in woodworking. From top to bottom: backsaw, coping saw, hacksaw, ripsaw, crosscut saw. To the left of the coping saw: keyhole saw.

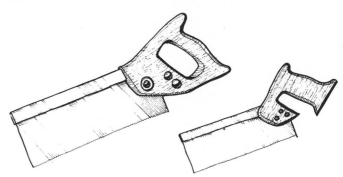

Figure II–11.
Backsaws are used in conjunction with the miter box. Both closed- and open-handled models are available.

Figure II–12.
The coping saw is used to make curved cuts in wood or plastic.

Hole Saw

This saw is used to cut large holes in wood. The hole saw has a drill bit centered on a cylindrical saw blade. Each set comes in a range of graduated sizes for various diameter holes. When using the hole saw, the center drill shaft is placed in the chuck of a portable electric drill or drill press. Adjust the tool for a slower speed and firmly bore the blade through the stock.

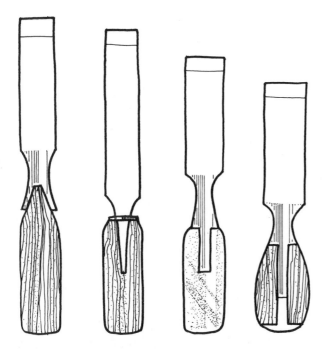

Figure II–13.
A variety of wood chisels used by the woodworker. Notice how the blade fits into an assortment of handles. Many of the handles can be replaced if the original is damaged or rendered useless due to continued wear and tear.

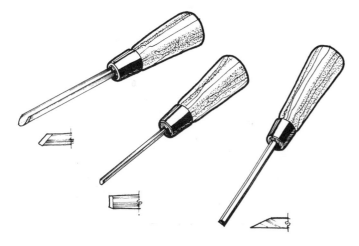

Figure II–14.
Wood-carving gouges. From left to right: Straight gouge, veiner gouge, straight-edge gouge.

CHISELS AND GOUGES

Chisels to be used by the woodworker are fitted with smoothly curved bulbous handles designed for a comfortable grip. The handles are usually made of hardwood or impact-resistant plastic. There is an assortment of sizes and tip configurations and each has specific functions in the carving of wood.

Firmer Chisel

This is a general-purpose wood-cutting tool with a blade approximately 4 inches long and rectangular in shape. A wooden- or leather-faced mallet is used to drive the wooden handled chisel; a hammer may be used on the plastic ones.

Butt Chisel

This is used for light woodworking. Light tapping with a hammer is possible. The blade is beveled on the top face of two long sides. It is excellent for creating undercuts in wood.

All-Steel Wood Chisel

This chisel is suitable for heavy woodwork and general carpentry. It is composed of a short, beveled edge blade and a hexagonal handle. It is a very sturdy tool that will withstand a good deal of abuse.

Firmer Gouge

Used to cut hollow or curved shoulders in wood, this tool is similar in construction to the firmer chisel, but differs in the shape of the blade, which is curved rather than straight. Two types are available—the out-cannel, which is used for deep hollow cutting, and the in-cannel, used for general cutting.

Scribing Gouge

Also called a "paring gouge," this tool is designed to be used with a mallet. Similar to the firmer gouge, this gouge has a longer handle, and, like the firmer gouge, it comes in a variety of blade sizes for various sized channels.

Mortise Chisel

The mortise chisel is used for light woodworking and to cut mortises in wood. It is usually made from thick steel with ends designed to be struck with a mallet. It is an excellent tool with which to work hardwoods.

Wood-turning Chisel and Gouge

Both of these tools are specifically designed to be used with wood fastened to a wood lathe. Both are extra long with handles made of hardwood. To minimize chatter and other vibrations a firm grip is essential to proper and safe use of the wood-turning tool, as the stock quickly rotates on the lathe. These tools are to be held in both hands with the blade resting on the lathe tool rest. One hand grips the uppermost portion of the blade, while the other hand grips the handle and steadies the tool when the lathe is in motion. Wood-turning chisels are sold under the following names—"diamond point" for V-grooving, "skew chisel" for beading, "round nose" for coving, "parting tool" for cutting to length.

Carving Gouge and Chisel

All carving chisels are ground on the outer face and are used for preliminary shaping with the mallet and, occasionally, by hand for more delicate cutting. Types available are the straight gouge, curved gouge, spoon-bit gouge, and the veiner gouge used for fine detail carving. Carving chisels are used to shape and finish work begun by carving gouges. Straight, curved, and spoon-bit chisels are the more common types.

PLANES

Planes are used to dimension and smooth lumber.

Jack Plane

The jack plane is used to dimension lumber by removing fine parings of wood by means of an adjustable blade used in conjunction with manual pressure. This is the most popular tool for general wood planing and should be durable in construction to withstand years of use.

Smoothing Plane

This is used for exact work on fairly short pieces of wood. The smoothing plane is made in 8- and 9-inch lengths. The cutting iron is mounted in the same way as the jack plane.

Jointer Plane

This tool is used to square long edges of lumber for jointing wood and is a very long tool in comparison with the jack and smoothing planes. It should be mentioned that all good planes are fully adjustable and made of strong steel and hardwood handles. The cutting iron or blade must be kept sharp at all times to maximize cutting effectiveness. Store the plane on its side and lightly grease bright metal parts to prevent rusting.

Block Plane

The block plane is used in one hand to smooth end grain and for other small jobs. It is 6 to 7 inches long.

Rasp Plane

The rasp plane is to be used to shape wood, plastic, and soft metals. Sometimes it is called a "Surform plane." The waste wood does not clog the teeth, but is easily cleared through holes in the cutting blade while the cutting process is underway. Lightweight and easy-to-replace blades make this a handy tool for many woodworking jobs.

Plow Plane

This is used to cut grooves and rabbets while being guided by fences and depth gauges.

Spokeshave

This is used to smooth curved wood. The tool is worked away from the body with a pushing motion. The reverse direction may be used.

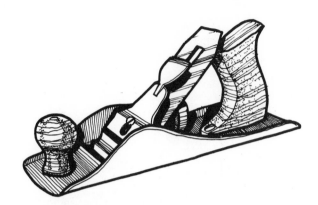

Figure II-15.
The jack plane is used to dimension lumber.

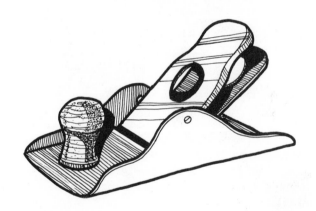

Figure II-16.
The block plane is used to trim end grain and other fine work.

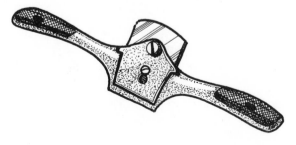

Figure II-17.
With a pushing motion, the spokeshave is used to smooth curved wood.

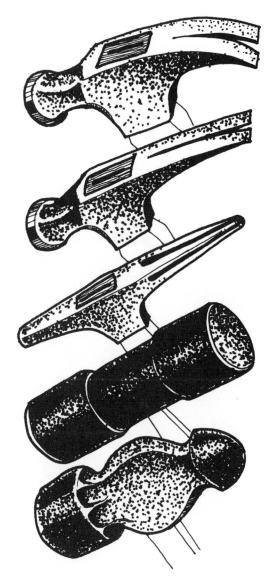

HAMMERS AND MALLETS

Hammers and mallets are of primary importance and are the most commonly used tools of woodworking. Although there are numerous types of hammers, each designed for a specific purpose, it is recommended that you obtain the three following types, and, if the opportunity presents itself, try other hammers, some of which are pictured in the illustration.

Claw Hammer

The claw hammer is used for nailing, withdrawing nails, and general carpentry.

Carver's Mallet

A carver's mallet is heavy in order to allow the craftsman to drive the chisel or gouge with short, controlled strokes, rather than driving blows. It is, in spite of its weight, relatively easy to hold and balance in the hand. The head is composed of beech or lignum vitae, two woods able to withstand a great deal of use.

Soft-Faced Mallet

The soft-faced mallet is used to drive or shape material that would be damaged by standard hammers and mallets. It is composed of rubber or leather with a handle of hardwood.

PLIERS

Depending on the type used, pliers can perform numerous jobs involving bending and gripping. Use pliers to prevent round stock from rolling when drilling.

Slip-Joint Pliers

These are standard pliers for removing or positioning small bits of wood or metal. They are a must for every craftsman's toolbox.

Snipe-Nosed Pliers

These are used to grip small objects in hard-to-reach places.

Figure II–18.
An assortment of hammers used in woodworking. From top to bottom: Claw hammer, roofer's claw hammer, upholsterer's hammer, rubber mallet, ballpeen hammer.

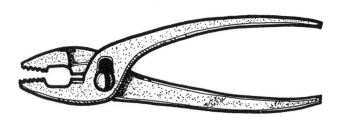

Figure II–20.
The standard pliers for carpentry.

Figure II–19.
A woodcarver's mallet is used to drive carver's chisels and gouges. It is usually made of beech or lignum vitae.

BRACES AND DRILLS

Braces and drills perform essentially the same function; that is, to bore holes in wood and to work in restricted space.

Brace

A brace is to be used in conjunction with an assortment of drill bits for boring holes in wood. The brace applies a turning force to the bit by rotation of the frame in a clockwise direction. It is a thoroughly handy tool dating back to early fifteenth-century Europe. Pressure is applied by means of the hand or by placing the swivel head on the front part of the body while either hand rotates the frame handle.

Hand Drill

The hand drill is used to drill holes in wood and metal. It is composed of a shaft to which gears are attached, providing a range of convenient speeds for different materials and types of work. The hand cranks one gear which sets the bit in motion for drilling. It is an advantageous tool for fine and exact drilling and is more desirable than the power drill in this respect.

Gimlet

The gimlet is used to bore shallow holes in lumber. Its size is 1/8 to 3/8 inch in diameter.

Bits

These are used in conjunction with the brace, hand drill, or power drill for boring holes. Consider obtaining two types—twist drill and dowel drill bits. Both drill holes. The twist drill has a pointed tip and is used for general drilling. The dowel bit has a spurred tip, which is useful for boring holes in side and end grains of wood and is designed to follow a straight line while drilling, as opposed to following the grain and wandering off center.

SCREWDRIVERS

Many hardware stores sell screwdrivers in kits, or they may be purchased individually. Either way, be sure your workshop is outfitted with the following: flared tip, Phillips head, Reed, and Prince. Flared tips should be of several sizes to accommodate various sizes of slotted-head screws. In addition, a ratchet screwdriver is handy for driving screws without altering the grip.

SANDERS AND ABRASIVES

Sandpaper and sanding blocks are essential to finishing wood properly. There are three categories of abrasives—coarse, medium, and fine, with further subdivisions in each category. True sandpaper, although not a misnomer, is no longer available; glass particles or flint are used in place of true sand.

Flint or Glasspaper

This is the cheapest sandpaper available, but it wears quickly and is to be used only for rough finishing.

Garnet

This is a natural red material used to finish all types of wood, including hardwood. It is harder than flint and is also available in finer grades. Garnet must be used dry, unlike some which may be used with oil or water.

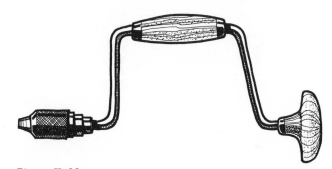

Figure II–22.
A hand brace is used to bore holes in wood.

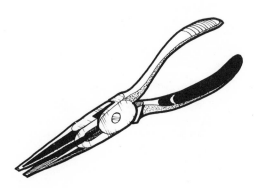

Figure II–21.
Snipe-nosed pliers, which are also referred to as needle-nosed pliers.

Figure II–23.
The gimlet is used to make shallow holes in lumber.

Emery

Emery is a very fine paper useful for extra-fine sanding. It clogs easily, but is advantageous for achieving a glasslike finish on many hardwoods. Paper- or cloth-backed types are available.

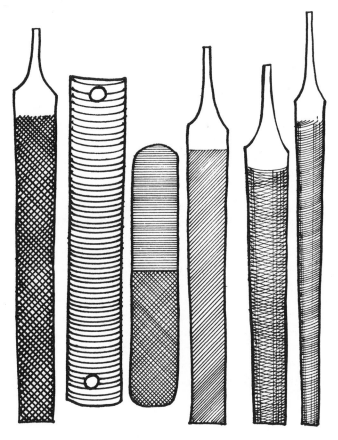

Figure II–24.
An assortment of wood and metal files. From left to right: flat double-cut file, curved tooth file, horse rasp, single-cut file, half-round double-cut file, round file.

Figure II–25.
The effects of file patterns on wood. Top from left to right: coarse single-cut, medium single-cut, fine single-cut. Bottom from left to right: coarse double-cut, medium double-cut, fine double-cut.

Sanding Block

A sanding block is used to finish flat surfaces. Sandpaper used without the aid of the block tends to follow any uneven surface of the wood or surface undulations. The sanding block, which is fitted with a core and sandpaper, is available commercially or one may be improvised. Simply select a block of scrap wood that will fit inside your hand and wrap the sandpaper around it. Rotate the sandpaper on the block as wearing or clogging takes place.

FILES

Files (and rasps too) are used to finish metal and wood, to remove burrs and irregularities, to enlarge holes and slots, and for a number of other jobs. They are classified by their cut, which is a direct result of how the teeth are formed and arranged on the face of the metal blade. The following comprise the most commonly preferred files in the workshop.

Flat File

The flat file is used to file flat surfaces on wood or metal. It is not to be used for filing inside curves. Single-cut (for fine work) and double-cut (for roughing) files are available. The double-cut bastard file is the coarsest of all.

Round File

The round file is used to file round holes or for curved surfaces. In some models the blade tapers toward the forward tip of the metal shank and this is useful for reaching into small places or for finishing concave surfaces. Round files are sometimes called "rat-tail files."

Half-Round File

The half-round file is for all-purpose filing. It combines the best features of the flat and round files. Use it for work on large circular areas.

Square File

To be used to file square holes or angles, the square file can also be used to file rectangular slots, keyways, and splines.

Needle Files

Used for precision filing work, needle files are small, delicate files. They are usually sold in sets containing rounds, flats, half-rounds, and triangular shapes. A useful assortment is well worth the nominal cost for a good set.

RASPS

Rasps, unlike files, have teeth designed primarily to remove very fine to medium slices or parings of wood. The bastard rasp gives a coarse cut while the smooth rasp is used for finer work. The usual shapes are flat, round, and half-round.

Surform Flat File

This is a relatively new tool of great versatility. It is lightweight and is an excellent tool for general filing. It performs the same job as the standard flat rasp. The blade is made of hardened steel and can be easily replaced.

Figure II–26.
A Surform wood rasp. A product of Stanley Tool Company, which can be used in place of the more traditional rasp. The Surform is very lightweight, sharp, and the blade can be replaced when worn.

Cabinet Rasp

Also known as a "wood rasp," this tool is designed with burrlike teeth for quick wood leveling or removal and is used in the preliminary steps prior to filing or finishing with sandpaper. It is available in flats, round, or half-rounds.

Rifflers

The riffler is used to file woodcarving. Rifflers are indeed craftsman's tools used for the finer detail work of convoluted and irregularly shaped projects. Some rifflers are double ended and bent, enabling them to be used in difficult-to-reach pockets and other areas of the project.

Power Tools

Each age brings with it new tools designed for specialization and economy of effort. The present day craftsman makes use of those tools that enable him to realize his plans and ideas in wood in the most complimentary way possible. The affinity between tools and their users must be a close one. Above all, the tool must not impinge itself on the user by making excessive demands in the way of maintenance, lubrication, adjustment; and continued internal repair. Electrical tools are usually more complex than their manual counterparts. However, they afford the user an unrivaled luxury in that they simplify the task at hand by minimizing physical strain and effort. These advantages alone make them highly useful in the woodworking process, and for this reason they should be considered as serious contenders in the tool marketplace. Today, power tools are in most cases inexpensive and within most budgets. A hand drill, saber saw, and circular saw, all outfitted with nominal accessories can be had for less

than seventy-five dollars. These are tools made by dependable manufacturers who take pride in their reputations.

Of course, one can make very fine wooden toys without the use of power tools whatsoever. Many of the world's finest toys were crafted in an era when power assisted tools had not yet become a sparkle in an inventor's eye. Particular delight is felt when a fine toy is made without the means of giant drill presses and radial-arm saws. The hand tool, manually operated or otherwise, seems to be more in scale with the user. Perhaps because it fits within the palm, it somehow becomes more of a natural extension of the hand, arm, and body. Consider the manually operated tool and its power tool counterpart carefully before you decide. Strive for a practical balance in your work area, incorporating each tool where it is useful in its own special way.

ELECTRIC DRILLS

Electric drills are sometimes referred to as "power drills." Used to drill holes in a wide range of materials with an assortment of readily available attachments, an electric drill performs a multitude of tasks. The chuck capacity to accommodate drill bits ranges from ¼ inch to 1¼ inch. Speed selection, reversing switches, drill size capacity, and general construction should all be considerations carefully weighed before you decide which drill to purchase. Search out useful attachments, such as drill stand, grindstone, buffing cloth, sander, and rasp and file fittings. Drill bits come in graduated sizes and are usually housed in a plastic container with each slot marked for drill bit placement or storage.

CIRCULAR SAWS

These are portable saws that are used to cut solid lumber and board to size. The saw is a highly useful tool with revolving blades of 6- to 10-inch diameter. It can be used for ripping or crosscutting at any angle, from 90 degrees down to 45 degrees. The depth of the cut can be adjusted from 0 to 2 3/16 inches on a 7-inch model. Thus you can use the saw for grooving and dadoing, as well as for sawing timbers. All portable circular saws should be fitted with a fixed upper blade guard and a lower blade guard, which is pushed back as the saw passes through the work. The lower guard is spring loaded and will quickly resume its noncutting position once the cut has been completed.

Blades are specifically designed for special jobs requiring a precise arrangement of teeth. The wrong blade can destroy a cherished piece of wood, as well as bring excessive wear prematurely to the blade and saw itself. Keep in mind that blades are best sharpened by a professional person who is equipped for such work. The following circular saw blades are recommended.

Rip Blade

The rip blade is used for cutting lumber parallel with the grain. It has pronounced teeth.

Crosscut Blade

This blade is designed to cut across the grain of solid lumber and is characterized by its fine, sharp teeth, evenly serrated.

Combination Blade

The combination blade is suitable for sawing lumber in any direction and for use while cutting particle or composition boards.

Flooring Blade

The flooring blade is to be used on secondhand lumber, especially when there is a risk of cutting through nails, screws, and other thin metal shafts.

SABER SAWS

These are in effect jigsaws driven by electric motors. The saw is fitted with straight, narrow blades, which can extend several inches below the base and move up and down in short strokes. Select the model that has variable speed selection. This tool is useful for cutting circles and other irregular shapes and for making inside cuts. Special files are available and can be used in place of the blade for sanding purposes. A guide fence, which easily attaches to the saw for more accurate cutting, is also a handy attachment.

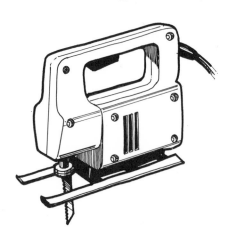

Figure II-27.
The saber saw is fitted with a straight and narrow blade. The tool is used for cutting circles and other irregular shapes and for making inside cuts.

BELT SANDERS

Belt sanders are used to sand wood quickly by means of an abrasive belt. This tool is recommended for those times when paint, varnish, and other superficial coatings must be quickly removed in order to expose the underlying wood. If coarse paper is used, it will abrade the wood surface considerably and, therefore, should be used with discretion. A dust bag can be attached to those models so equipped making them ideal for environments where dust in the air is a nuisance. Sand the wood with the grain, exerting just enough pressure to achieve the desired results.

Inordinate pressure will cause the motor to overheat and will slow the belt action. Keep several grades of sandpaper handy for finer work and refinishing.

Workbenches

A good workbench is a "must" item for any woodworker, cabinetmaker, or wood sculptor. Any woodworker who has had to work on an unstable surface will attest to this. The following are key requirements for any good bench.

1. Sturdiness achieved by weight and quality of construction.
2. The ability to hold your work in a variety of positions by means of clamps, vises, or bench dogs.
3. A large, smooth work surface.
4. An adequate tool tray.

In order to help you do hand work with confidence, it is suggested that any table you make or purchase meet the above critera. Space available for your wood projects will help you decide the overall dimensions of your table. Although it is not necessary to paint or varnish the workbench, all surfaces should be sanded from top to bottom. Many workbenches are fastened to the weight-bearing studs of the inner garage wall. This enables the bench to be made sturdily and remain fixed. Hardwood, such as oak, maple, ash, or birch, are ideal woods to be used in the construction of both the underpinning frame and the tabletop.

WOODWORKING BENCHES

The underframe of the woodworking bench should be constructed of heavy-duty 2 by 4 s and 4 by 4s. The top should be flat and capable of withstanding heavy blows. An end vise may be installed to provide clamping facilities. The woodworking bench is sometimes called a "cabinetmaker's bench."

Figure II-28.
Constructed of heavy-duty lumber, the workbench is an essential piece of furniture in the shop.

Figure II-29.
The Workmate bench made by Stanley Power Tools, is lightweight and collapsible. Reasonable in price, the bench is ideal for small piece work.

WORKMATE BENCH

Workmate benches are collapsible, which makes them relatively portable for purposes of storage or transporting. They are usually adjustable to two levels, offering a convenient height for sawing lumber and boards. These devices are reasonable in price and are becoming more popular among woodworking hobbyists. Local hardware stores and home improvement centers stock or can order for you.

Miscellaneous Tools

The following tools are items that facilitate working with wood. They should be included in the shop and can easily be stored in drawers beneath the workbench or, in some cases, hung on a pegboard.

MITER BOXES

A miter box is a jig device which guides the blade of a back saw to cut wood at 45-degree miters or 90-degree squared ends. Simple in construction, this device is useful for making frames or cutting wood where angles need to be made accurately. The simplest version is made of wood

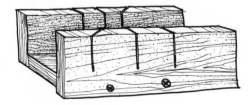

Figure II-30.
A miter box is an inexpensive jig device used to guide the blade of a backsaw to cut wood at 45 and 90 degrees.

and is dimensioned like a shoe box with slots that have been precut.

PROTECTIVE GOGGLES

Made of high-impact plastic, goggles, or their counterpart, face shields, are required for any wood work where there is even the remotest possibility that injury to the eye or other parts of the face may occur. They are an absolute must when working with power tools and equipment. They should be distortion free, clear, and should have replaceable plastic lenses.

CARPENTER'S SCRIBES

These provide a more reliable line on wood than do pencil points, which dull and frequently are imprecise. The scribe is made adjustable by means of loosening the thumbscrew, which is mounted on the side.

SAFETY DUST MASKS

The masks protect against nuisance dust and nontoxic paint sprays. If you wear glasses, find a mask that is comfortable to wear with them. Replaceable filters are available on most kinds.

GLOVES

Although not necessary to wear when handling milled stock, gloves do service to the user when splintered or weather-beaten wood is to be cut, shaped, stripped, etc. The better ones are made of leather; some have cloth backs and a leather face on the palm side.

LIGHTING

Lighting for good visibility is best achieved with fluorescent fixtures mounted directly above the work area. A gooseneck lamp mounted near or on the bench for small detailed work is an excellent additional source of illumination. The lamp must be out of harm's way and should be positioned adjacent to the immediate work area.

Floor-Standing Power Tools

These tools are usually reserved for the serious woodworking craftsman and can be of immense service for work involving extensive cutting, sanding, and other means of wood preparation. If your wooden toys begin to approach assembly line proportions through your generosity or sheer demand, consider adding one or more of the following pieces of equipment to your stable of tools. These tools are expensive. Sales in major department or hardware stores are worth waiting for; the price reduction can be considerable.

DRILL PRESSES

These are used to drill holes in wood, plastic, and metal. The drill press is simply a more accurate version of the hand drill or power drill. Numerous adjustments can be made for repeated precision drilling. An adjustable shaft and metal stage or table takes much of the guesswork out of drilling. The drilling head incorporates a rear-mounted motor which can be geared to turn faster or slower by means of graduated pulleys and the connecting rubber belt. Any drill bit used with the portable power drill is suitable for use on the drill press. Stock can be fixed on the metal table to free one hand to perform other functions.

RADIAL-ARM SAWS

In radial-arm saws the motor and circular saw blade are suspended from an arm that swings out over the worktable at any angle and that can be adjusted up and down to accommodate different thicknesses of wood. The saw can be fitted with various attachments to cut dadoes, grooves, rabbets, joints, and moldings. Because the saw blade swivels from side to side and also tilts from vertical to horizontal, the machine offers great flexibility. The blades range from 8 to 20 inches in diameter. The most versatile blade to be used with the radial-arm saw is the combination blade. The saw blade can be replaced by a cutter head which takes two or three shaped knives. The cutter head fits on the saw arbor and is useful for cutting edge joints and various types of molding. It is possible to cut tongue and groove fittings as well. Drilling can also be done by fitting a chuck on the opposite end of the arbor from the saw blades.

TABLE SAWS

These shop saws are waist high, stationary, and designed for precision cutting of wood and medium-sized panels of plywood. Like other electrically driven shop tools table saws are the mainstays of furniture and cabinetmakers. The motor is mounted beneath a metal table with the adjustable blade projecting up through a slot in the table. The work is fed into the saw, which cuts on the downstroke. Blade sizes are 8, 9, 10, or 12 inches in diameter and are available for ripping, crosscutting, or combination service. The blade can be tilted to bevel a board. By substituting a dado head or molding head, dadoes and molding cuts are possible. As handy as the table saw is, it represents a sizable and rather dubious purchase for the hobbyist, unless you plan to cut large pieces of wood in great amounts. Even then, the radial-arm saw is the more versatile tool of the two.

BAND SAWS

Band saws are designed to convert large sections of lumber to size and to cut curves in a variety of materials, from thin woods to stock up to 6 inches thick. A band saw is a power tool that is widely used in industry to cut lumber to size, particularly where curves are involved. Smaller versions manufactured for home use are available. The blade is a toothed steel hoop which is driven around two wheels inside the metal casing to give a continuous cutting edge.

BENCH JIGSAWS

Sometimes called "scroll saws," bench jigsaws are particularly useful for cutting curves in thinner woods. This is known as scroll work. The saw is capable of cutting angles of small radii. The main advantage of this saw is that it leaves both hands free to guide the work. Fitted with the correct blade, it can handle straight cuts in work up to approximately 2 inches thick. It is best placed on a worktable surface. It takes up very little space because of its overall dimensions. Optional floor stands are available.

Glues

The use of fast- and slow-drying, transparent, permanent glues is an important factor for all types of woodworking. Today's technology brings with it new glues which do not necessarily spell an improvement over the more tried and true glues that have been in use for hundreds of years. Clearly, you must experiment with the range of glues on the market today. Over the years, I have decided upon certain requirements that must be met before I use a particular glue for a project. Start out by asking some basic questions. What kind of abuse is the toy to get? Here the important factor is the strength of the bond of the woods and whether it will hold up with continued use. Is the toy likely to be exposed to water or extreme dampness? A nonwater-resistant glue used in wood construction and lamination may cause the wood to delaminate or simply fall apart if no other external or internal pinning or bonding is employed. Will the glue stain the wood? How long does it take to dry and fully cure? Shelf life, clean-up, and appropriate solvents must also be considered. A few woods, because of their oily nature, require special glue. Teak is one of these woods.

Making strong glue joints with glues applied in liquid form depends primarily upon a proper balance between gluing pressure and the consistency of the glue during pressing. The glue mixture, once it is spread on the wood, is variable. The proper bonding of woods depends upon such factors as the kind of glue, quality of the glue, moisture content of the wood, temperature of the glue and room, the time between spreading and pressing, and the extent to which the glue-coated surfaces are exposed to the air. To ensure a strong joint in wood a thin layer of glue, unbroken by air bubbles or small foreign particles, should be in contact with the wood surfaces over the entire joint area.

Pressure should be used to squeeze the glue out into a thin continuous film between the wood layers, to force air from the joint, to bring the wood surfaces into intimate contact with the glue, and to hold them in this position for the duration of the setting and curing process. The strongest joints usually result when the consistency of the glue permits the use of moderately high pressures.

Clamps or other means of exerting pressure on the wood should be left intact, until they can overcome the interior stresses of the wood. This applies whether the wood is warped, very porous, or irregular in form. Many woods have a springlike quality to them, which usually poses no real problem to the woodworker. However, it still is the job of the glue to hold the wood together in spite of these obstacles. Here again, experience with the glues listed and with various woods will provide you with the necessary information to continue building a variety of both large and small toys, whether they are made of two or ten pieces of wood.

The following woodworking glues are recommended. Each has its own unique properties and qualities, all of which should be taken into consideration when the gluing phase of construction is approached. Whether it will be easy or difficult to obtain a satisfactory joint depends upon the density of the wood, the structure of the wood, the presence of fillers, and the type of glue used. Generally, heavy woods are more difficult to glue than lightweight woods; hardwoods are more difficult to glue than softwoods; and heartwood is more difficult than sapwood. However, these differences can be minimized if you do the following:

1. Prepare the wood properly for a smooth, tight fit, which will yield a better bond.
2. Use glue of good quality, making sure that it has been prepared and mixed properly just prior to its application.
3. Closely follow the details of the gluing process set forth in the procedural instructions for each toy.
4. Clamp tightly, allow to set in a dry environment, and always wait until glue is fully dried and cured.

ANIMAL HIDE

General Characteristics: This is a time-honored glue (made from animal hides and bones), having long been used extensively in woodworking. It is extremely strong and long lasting and does not become brittle with age. Thin coats of it must be applied to both surfaces and then allowed to become tacky before joining.

Drying time: Sets rapidly, five to fifteen minutes, at a temperature of 72 degrees Fahrenheit or above.

Uses: Joint work where there is no exposure to water.

Application: Must be applied while very warm; better if applied hot.

Note: If you are using the liquid pre-prepared form, follow the manufacturer's instructions. If you choose to purchase the cake form, soak in cold water, then heat in glue pot to 140 degrees and keep at this temperature for several hours before glue can be used for bonding or joinery work. Six to eight hours is not an unreasonable time. The cold type of glue may be applied directly from the bottle. It's better if applied warm, however.

PLASTIC RESIN

General Characteristics: This is a relatively new glue on the market (made from minute resin particles) in the ready-to-use plastic bottle form. It is very strong and has very high water resistance, but is not altogether waterproof. Do not use it with oily woods, and keep in mind that it becomes brittle if joint fits poorly. If used with pegs and/or dowels, they must fit snugly.

Drying Time: Sets up hard enough to work within 5 to 6 hours. Clamping is an absolute necessity. Thorough curing requires twenty-four to forty-eight hours or longer if moisture or dampness is present.

Uses: Use in joint work and lamination.

Application: Apply cold.

EPOXY

General Characteristics: This is an excellent glue (made from resin) for the bonding of wood with dissimilar materials, such as metal, glass, plastic, etc. It is strong, resists heat, and must be used with a catalyst hardener usually provided with the purchase. Follow manufacturer's instructions.

Drying time: Sets overnight. Sets more rapidly if placed in a warm room, but expect it to take up to twenty-four hours for best results.

Uses: Use for joining wood to wood, and wood to china, metal, or glass.

Application: Apply cold, once it has been properly mixed with hardener.

CONTACT CEMENT

General Characteristics: This is a liquid ready-mixed for use. It becomes extremely tacky with setting and the glue is not easily adjusted while drying process is underway. Its water resistance is very high and it is an excellent material for projects requiring lamination of veneer or thin pieces of wood. A light-duty glue of moderate strength, it is usually used for large surface bonding, such as wall paneling and Formica tops.

Drying time: Sets in thirty minutes. It must be allowed to become tacky before use. Complete drying usually takes eighteen to twenty-four hours in a warm room.

Uses: Excellent for bonding of wood to leather, thin laminates, and soft, porous materials. It is lightly colored.

Application: Apply cold, direct from can. Apply to both surfaces before clamping or applying weights.

RESORCINOL RESIN

General Characteristics: This is a one hundred percent waterproof glue of great strength. Several brands are available in liquid form with the catalyst supplied separately. Some brands are combinations of phenol and resorcinol resins. It is relatively high-priced.

Drying Time: May still be worked in the first thirty to sixty minutes. Drying takes up to 20 hours, but can be accelerated in warm or even hot environments.

Uses: Primarily for gluing lumber or assembly joints that must withstand severe service conditions. May affect the color of the wood because of staining properties. Excellent for toys to be used outdoors.

Application: Apply thin coats to both surfaces, use clamps. Quickly remove visible residue to avoid stains.

WHITE GLUE

General Characteristics: An excellent all-around glue (made from liquid resin) which is readily available in small to large containers. It is inexpensive, nonstaining, nontoxic, and good for small assemblies provided clamping of some type is used (string, rubber bands, tape, etc.). Water soluable and quick setting, this glue is a favorite among beginning woodworkers because of its carefree nature and ease of cleanup.

Drying time: Sets in twenty to thirty minutes with moderate pressure. Allow twenty-four hours for best results. Moisture will retard drying time.

Uses: Good for bonding of wood to wood, or wood to paper, fabric, canvas, felt, cork; used for light-strength gluing to plastic.

Application: To be applied directly from container. Do not allow glue to become warm, as this will precipitate drying. Both surfaces need not be covered with the glue. Spread the glue with brush or cardboard scraps, using finger to apply glue in hard-to-reach places or on contoured wood.

CASEIN

General Characteristics: Several brands of casein (made from milk curd) are sold in dry powder form; it may also be prepared from raw materials. It has a high to low dry strength and low resistance to water. However it is moderately durable under damp conditions. The glue has a pronounced dulling effect on tools and will stain some woods.

Uses: Good on oily woods and works well when cool. Must be mixed for each use. Good for joint work as a filler. If prepared from powdered form, it must be mixed in equal volume with water and continuously stirred.

Drying time: Drying takes from four to six hours at 72 degrees.

Application: Apply cold with a thin coat on each surface to be joined. Moderate clamping is optional, but helps to reduce air pockets.

Finishes

The appearance of wood can be appreciated from two viewpoints—its natural state and its finished state. In its natural state, once it has been milled and made available to the consumer, it has all the features that make it distinctive and unlike other materials. It possesses character, raw color, and unique physical properties—some desirable for one job and undesirable for another. In its finished state, the natural qualities and properties of the wood are often enhanced by the finish, which brings out the beauty of the grain, highlights, and inherent tones. Finishing the wood protects it from moisture, dirt, stain and prolongs its life.

Every craftsman who works with wood is faced with decisions. "How shall I finish the wood?" "How smooth, how shiny, how light, or how dark is the wood to be?" "What is the effect I want the wood to have when I complete my work?" And, when the craftsman has come to some conclusions, the next question is "What are the means to accomplish my task?" The choice of a finish or the very lack of one is the responsibility of each wood artist. Therefore, it must be realized that the choice is governed not only by personal taste, but by how well the particular wood lends itself to the chosen finish. This is further compounded by the very real and practical side of the matter; that is, how the object is to be used.

Several considerations combined with wise selection of material will help produce the best union of all these.

Regardless of which type of wood or finish is in question, the following are rules you should follow:

1. Finish wood in a dust-free room away from possible contamination.
2. Use the best materials for the job commensurate with affordability.
3. Experiment on scrap materials before proceeding to finish the actual toy.
4. Evaluate the number of possible ways the toy is to be used, whether it is to be subjected to a great deal of wear and tear or more likely to be displayed for its more sculptural and aesthetic qualities.
5. Experiment with a wide variety of finishes and make note of your observations and conclusions, if any.
6. Before applying any clear finish or finishing material, for that matter, use a tack rag (commercially available) to remove dust, small wood particles, and other foreign material.

The first step in the finishing process is to apply stain, if desired, to change the color or bring out the grain. Stain is applied to the raw wood and penetrates the surface (to a greater or lesser degree depending upon the kind of stain). It will not penetrate evenly if other substances, such as glue, have been used, so make your decision regarding stain in the planning stages of your toy making, as it may be advisable to stain some pieces before they are assembled.

The final finishing agents recommended here are those which provide a clear film on the surface of the wood, adding luster and a protective coating. Wax, oil, shellac, varnish, or lacquer may be used, each having advantages and disadvantages. In general, wax or oil provide less protection and permanence, but give a warm, natural glow to the wood. Shellac, varnish, or lacquer, applied in several thin coats, will build up a hard protective surface, which will reveal the beauty of the natural wood and withstand years of use. Some of these finishes can be combined or used in succession, some cannot. Manufacturer's instructions and the general information which follows should answer your basic questions.

WAX

Hard carnauba paste wax is recommended. A gentle heating of both wax and surface will accelerate penetration of the first coat. Allow to dry for approximately one hour and remove with a stiff fiber brush that will not mar the wood. Apply successive coats and polish with cheesecloth. A final buffing should be done with an even softer cloth, such as a diaper, terry cloth, or the underside of a discarded sweatshirt. The waxing process should not be hurried. It is an activity that is the fruit of the craftsman's hard labor and provides the penultimate touch in woodworking. One or more coats of wax may be applied as a final step when finishing with sealers or protective agents.

OIL

Oil is best prepared in a double boiler. Heat equal parts of linseed oil and turpentine to 80 degrees Fahrenheit. (WARNING: This material is highly flammable and should be handled under strict supervision.) Slowly stir the two ingredients and apply with a soft brush or rag. Allow the oil solution to penetrate the wood. Wipe off the excess oil with several passes of a clean cloth. Apply further coats, several times the first day, following the same procedure. Repeat this process once daily for a week, once weekly for a month, and once monthly for a year. This aging process will bring out the full, deep color and luster of any wood. It is a slow and long process, but one of the best ways to bring to the surface the deeper richness of wood. It also seasons the wood for ultimate durability.

VARNISH–OIL

Prepare the wood in the usual way. Mix equal parts of boiled linseed oil, turpentine, and spar-varnish. The spar varnish is used when there is likely to be such abuses as scratching or nicking or excessive contact with water. It dries very hard and is not easily affected by conditions just mentioned. Warm the liquid to 70 degrees Fahrenheit. Apply with a smooth, lint-free cloth in the direction of the grain. Allow a few minutes for the mixture to penetrate the grain. Then continue to rub vigorously until the wood's surface will no longer accept the oil. With another piece of cloth, wipe the surface until all signs of wetness have disappeared. Varnish-oil must be worked quickly to prevent streaking. Allow the toy to stand for a week to ten days before applying a coat or two of wax for further protection.

SHELLAC

Shellac, a substance in use since the fifteenth century, can be finicky if not worked properly. Old shellac spoils if left on the shelf too long, and, when applied in this condition,

renders the wood surface tacky and rarely fully cures. It is not waterproof or alcohol-proof, and it should not be used where the toy may be in contact with heat, as discoloration occurs. It is stored at room temperature and does not adhere to lacquered, waxed, or enameled surfaces. In spite of these disadvantages, shellac is very durable, elastic, and strong. It gives wood a beautiful finish and is fast drying. Purchase it in one-time-use quantities and make sure it is fresh when you buy it. The color of natural shellac is orange and is therefore used on darker woods so that any tint the shellac may carry with it will be hidden. White shellac, also commercially available, is bleached to permit its use on light-colored woods. Some of the strength of the white shellac is lost due to its processing and, like the orange, it must be used within a short period.

It is recommended that you finish your project with several layers of one-pound-cut shellac (the "cut" being the amount of lac dissolved in the alcohol base), rather than one coat of three- to four-pound-cut shellac. The latter is too thick and exacts its own kind of penance if used without discretion. You can make one-pound shellac by mixing four parts alcohol with three parts of three-pound-cut shellac. Apply with a fine-bristled brush of animal composition. A nylon brush is not impervious to the chemical substances contained within the shellac thinned with alcohol. Shellac is an excellent sealer and one coat can serve as a good base for varnish or lacquer.

LACQUER

Lacquer is used when a fast-drying finish is required. It is synthetic and is available in two consistencies—one for brushing, the other for spraying. Either way it can be thinned according to the manufacturer's instructions. Lacquer has a peculiar way of leeching color from previously stained woods and causes bleeding of the color. It can also actually cause bleeding of the natural color of the wood, unless the wood has been previously sealed with a lacquer sanding-sealer. Manufacturers have long been cognizant of this aberrant effect and now make a line of bleed-resistant stains and wood fillers to obviate this problem.

Brush lacquer can be used on larger designs where flat surfaces and the lack of tight crevices allow for a smooth application. However, because it dries so quickly, it is easier and generally more successful to apply lacquer by spraying (using either compressed air equipment or an aerosol can). Lacquer dries to a very clear, almost invisible film (unless one is chosen that has a coloring agent to mask the wood to some degree). It is moisture and heat resistant. When the finish is thoroughly dry, a coat or two of wax can be added for a higher gloss. Shellac can be used as an undercoat, but do not apply lacquer over varnish, paint, or a penetrating oil stain.

VARNISHES

Varnish is another transparent finishing and preservative agent. It has long been in use. The Egyptians used it to decorate their tombs; the Greeks employed it as a wood preservative to protect their ships from the corrosive effects of the sea and its elements. In fact, it is only during the last few centuries that varnish came into widespread use as a furniture finish.

The advantage to using varnish is the hard drying property it brings with it when properly applied to wood surfaces. Chemically, it is not as simple a substance as shellac and is available in several forms for the woodworker.

When applying varnish room temperature should be between 70 and 80 degrees Fahrenheit. The room should be dust-free and traffic-free. Clean the wood surface thoroughly with benzene to remove all traces of oil, dirt, grease, and other foreign substances. Repeat this procedure in between applied coats of the varnish, as well. If any sanding has been performed, use a tack rag to lift loose particles that have inadvertently come into contact with the surface.

Do not stir the varnish. This causes bubbles, which may in turn be transferred to the wood surface and harden. If the varnish appears too thick, run warm water over the can for a few minutes to bring the varnish to a thinner consistency for better flow. Brush with the grain until the entire area is covered. Assorted brushes of different sizes make the task of reaching difficult areas easier. Cross-grain varnishing may be attempted after the first pass with the grain by applying less pressure and by working off the tips of the bristles in a light-stroking manner.

After the varnish has completely dried, sand with 500 wet/dry sandpaper before applying the next coat. Use the tack rag after each sanding session.

Rub the final coat when dry with powdered pumice and oil or rottenstone with a small amount of water. These are both very fine grit abrasives and are to be used with discretion. Too much rubbing can wear away the top layer of finish and result in an uneven surface.

The following varnishes vary in terms of drying time, surface gloss, and resistance to moisture.

Oil Varnish

Oil varnish contains natural resins or gums (which serve as the body), oil (such as linseed oil, which serves as the vehicle), turpentine thinner, and a drying agent (to speed up the drying process). Drying time in room temperature is about twenty-four hours. The environment of the varnished item must be controlled for humidity, temperature, and dust particles, which are likely to settle on finishes that are somewhat tacky and will remain this way for an extended period of time. These shortcomings have been offset by synthetic resin varnish, a newer product, which also cuts down the drying period.

Cabinet Varnish

An all-around, versatile varnish with a high degree of resin, it dries with a hard surface and can be rubbed to a high gloss when aided by an appropriate rubbing powder, such as rottenstone. Cabinet varnish is an excellent alternative to the polyurethane or lacquer materials, while having the advantage of easy spreadability.

Flat Varnish

A varnish that dries with a dull, flat appearance, flat varnish requires no rubbing and is usually applied over a full gloss varnish to give the dulling effect. It lacks a hand-rubbed appearance and is notably lackluster in its overall effect, which may be desirable when a protective coating is needed for the project, but a glossy, or hand-rubbed surface is disdained.

Exterior Spar Varnish

This varnish is suitable for use on wood that must be made waterproof. It is long in drying time, flows easily, and provides an excellent protective coating on the surface. It has an elastic quality, which makes it unacceptable if hand-rubbing to achieve a luster is desired. While no other undercoating may be used, several coats of exterior spar varnish may be used to build up the finish.

Interior Spar Varnish

This is to be used with toys that will be subjected to extensive abuse. It is used as a bar surfacing and sealing liquid and can be rubbed to a satin gloss, but will not take on a high gloss sheen. This material should be considered a low priority material for the finishing of the small toys suggested in this book.

Polyurethane Varnish

Manufactured under several trade names, the most common of which is Varithane, polyurethane varnish produces an extremely tough and flexible finish on wood surfaces. It is fast-drying, relatively dustfree, and can be rubbed with 0000 steel wool within five to six hours to cut the glossy surface.

GLAZES

Glazes are color pigments combined with a sealer or varnish vehicle. They can be used to bring a slight degree of earth tone color to woods and are regarded as a coloring agent rather than a penetrating stain. A simple vehicle can easily be mixed by combining eight parts of satin varnish, two parts of boiled linseed oil, and one part of turpentine. Add desired pigment to produce the degree of color for the job. With a clean brush or lint-free cloth, apply the glaze in thin coats to the surface and then selectively remove portions to achieve an aged or highlighted effect.

MAKING
THE TOYS

It should be said at the outset that there are several ways to approach the designing and tooling of the following projects, or any other project for that matter. Once the idea has been conceived, get the main points down on paper. These fleeting thoughts need not be labored over, nor do they in any way have to resemble finished blueprints. The objective for marking down the salient features of the toy is to work out the features and intended function of the toy. Does the toy move, create noises or musical sounds? What is a workable scale? And, equally important, how do you initially see it being put together?

Try to imagine an exploded view of the toy as I have attempted to portray in the projects illustrated in the following pages. This can be a very important element in visualizing the overall appearance the toy is to have. Don't fret over the specific types of wood to be used at this point. That pleasurable aspect of woodcrafting can come later.

Once a workable plan is noted, proceed to make further notes on the construction as they come to mind. I have found that making a rapid visualization of the toy on a large sheet of paper helps make some of the unintentional errors and problems all the more glaring. An outline of the way I plan to proceed in making the toy then follows. All thoughts, half-baked or thought through, are made on this large sheet. Space is reserved on the plan for itemizing tools and other necessary materials. A place for wood selection is also set aside. This part of the planning is followed by a search for appropriate wood presently on hand as opposed to going out and purchasing different species to offset the wood I do not have.

Making a Pattern

Once you have thought the project through and made notes, rework your drawing until it suits you. Then make drawings of each view of the toy to be used as patterns for cutting the wood (i.e., top, bottom, side, front, back, as required). You can draw these patterns the exact size you want the finished product to be, or do them in any convenient size and then enlarge or reduce them to the finished size by one of the following methods:

THE GRID METHOD
This is the classic method of sketching a pattern. A grid is first drawn on a piece of paper or on the original pattern. (If drawn on a separate sheet, it is then laid on top of the pattern.) A similar grid, scaled to suit the final size desired, is drawn on another sheet of paper. The places where major outlines of the original pattern intersect lines of the overlaid grid are noted and then marked on the second grid at the same relative points. Sketching out the idea then becomes a fairly simple matter of connecting the marked points with short sketch lines.

THE SLIDE PROJECTION METHOD
Using slide film, photograph the original pattern sketches. Process the film and then project the slide on a wall to which you have taped a large sheet of paper. Move the projector closer or further away un-

til the projected image is the size you want. Trace the major lines of the form on the paper.

THE OPAQUE PROJECTOR METHOD

An overhead or opaque projector is used to enlarge the sketch and to project the new size on a sheet of paper. Overhead projectors can be rented from sources such as camera stores and artist-supply companies. Some public libraries will make them available for a nominal charge.

Transferring the Pattern Onto the Wood

Rub powdered graphite on the back of the pattern pieces and lay the paper over the wood's surface. Retrace the lines on the paper, and, in effect, a carbon-paper-type of tracing is made onto the wood. If the pieces are quite simple, you can transfer the measurements to the wood and mark your cutting lines without the need for paper patterns.

Making a Model

On occasion, I have found it very helpful to make a small or full-scale model or prototype of the toy to check to see if it does what I expect it to do. This way, if the toy doesn't work, looks awkward, or is less than satisfactory in some way, then all that is wasted is scrap material. In the long run, I find this procedure to be more fruitful. Initially, starting to make the toy with the more precious material might be intimidating to the novice, and even to the more experienced craftsman.

This may also be the time when you discover some aspect of the toy that did not show itself during the preliminary stages of thinking and drawing. For example, the wooden hobbyhorse pictured in one section of this book was originally conceived without the small, free-rolling wheel that it now has. The wheel came about only as an afterthought when it occurred to me that a wheel attached to the bottom of the dowel rod would make travel with the toy simpler and would prevent it from making grooves in our new linoleum.

This is also the time to test out the toy. Mind you, I feel no chagrin when it comes time to test a toy, even if it is meant for a younger, smaller person. Test it thoroughly and then make necessary adjustments to improve the overall mechanics of how it moves, clicks, spins, or performs any number of intended functions.

Gathering Tools and Materials

When you are ready to begin construction of the toy (or prototype) the first step is to set out the tools and materials you will need. Having these visible and within reach saves the nuisance of having to look for something in the middle of a process. Make your final wood choices and transfer your patterns to the appropriate surfaces.

Cut any large pieces of wood to rough size, always allowing enough extra for the final shaping. There is nothing more frustrating than trying to work with a piece cut too small, so provide plenty of margin. If you are going to laminate your wood (see instructions), cut the individual pieces to rough size.

Once the wood has been cut, decide what glues you will need and scrutinize those on hand for freshness. If there is any question, mix up a new batch. Gluing is such an essential and integral part of woodwork that it only invites trouble to gamble with glues that have hardened, separated, or become unworkable. Glue is the one bonding element that serves to unify the toy and keep it together despite repeated use and abuse.

Once the glue, glue brush, wood, and tools are on hand, then carefully review your drawing and see if it still sets well with you. Minor changes can be made as you proceed.

Laminating

If you intend to laminate your wood, now is a good time to begin this phase of toy making. If you have selected a glue that requires lengthy drying time, you can glue, clamp, and set the laminated piece aside. Meanwhile, work can be underway on other parts of the toy while it is drying.

Before gluing, consider whether you want to stain any of the wood that is to be laminated. If so, staining before gluing is advisable. Glue is absorbed into the pores of the wood very quickly, and, if the glue is in the pores, stain will not penetrate quickly. This might cause uneven coloration.

It is important to plan the clamping in detail prior to the gluing operation. Before the glue is actually applied to the wood, place the wood in the clamp to be sure it will fit without binding. If you need to improvise your clamping procedure because the clamps you have are inadequate for a particular job, determine your needs ahead of time. Once glue is applied to the wood you should be able to proceed quickly and confidently. When everything is ready, apply the glue, position the wood, and clamp it.

Adjust clamps occasionally, as air pockets and residual glue are forced out from beneath or in between the woods. Tight clamping will assure you of the best possible joining. Use a sufficient amount of glue to hold the joint well, yet little enough to prevent pieces from sliding or becoming too messy when they are clamped together, forcing most of the glue out of the joint. All residual glue should be cleaned off the wood immediately. Some glues (contact cement, mastic) become very rubbery as they begin to cure and are best left to become tacky before removing.

Sawing, Shaping, and Fitting the Pieces Together

Decide upon the best means of sawing the wood. The coping saw or its electric counterparts, the band saw or jigsaw, should be used to rough out the basic forms. Tight curves and radii are best avoided on the first pass through the blade. Continued refinement is only possible once the more bulky forms are removed. If you are using the coping saw, place the wood in the vice and tightly secure it without marring the surface (by means of the bench stops, if your table is equipped with these). A standard wood clamp and occasionally a metal vise can be employed to squeeze the pieces of wood together. Proceed slowly, sawing with gradual pressure, being careful not to push the blade beyond its limits. You may need to remove the clamps to disengage the waste from the usable portion of the wood block or to rearrange the stock to give you a better angle to more accurately cut into the deeper portions.

Shaping of the wood is best accomplished by means of a rasp or file of one shape or another. This is the case with contoured wood that has many undulations or hills and valleys. Flat wood, of course, is best levelled by means of jack plane or belt sander. Periodically, compare your burgeoning work with your drawings to keep an accurate tab as to whether it conforms to your chosen scale, form, etc.

When using the rasp, use both hands to remove unwanted peaks by allowing the tool to shave the surfaces in a gradual fashion. If abraded too abruptly, especially across the grain, the wood may splinter, leaving an undesirable groove in the surface. Sculpting the wood by the subtractive process will give you some feeling for the natural convexities and concavities of the form. To eliminate unwanted bumps and dents, try steaming the area. This will cause swelling, raising the surface to where bumps can be more easily ground off or left to dry, filling out the hollow portions.

Cracks or checks uncovered by sawing or shaping are to be filled with a matching wood filler or wood putty. Wood filler is composed of small particles of a particular type of wood and mixed with a paste. The filler is forced into the crack with the finger or some other tool. The filler may have different staining properties than the solid wood and will, therefore, stain darker. If this is the case, wood bleach can lighten the filler with wax toners being applied afterwards to more closely match wood colors.

Wood fillers need not dismay the woodworker. Unforeseen fissures, checks, and splits often appear only after the wood has been sufficiently worked to make them visible. The natural appeal of the wood far outweighs any natural flaws. The wood artist will often integrate the defect into the design visually reinforcing the wood's inherent properties. Each material has its own special qualities; and, while wood can often be unpredictable, it is alive, warm, and gives a sense of growth, unlike plastic, metal and synthetic materials.

If the toy you have chosen to build needs to have holes drilled in it, parts morticed, or channels cut after the forms have been blocked out, then clamp the wood so that both hands are free to work the tools best designed to shape the final touches prior to sanding. The sanding action will further smooth the surface to bring out a deep lustre for which wood is venerated.

Finishing

Begin sanding with a coarse paper, gradually working through medium and fine grades before waxing and polishing. The application of oils, wax, and stains has already been covered in this book.

There is a distinction between rough sanding and fine finishing, which are both accomplished with abrasive papers used on sanding blocks, grinders, disc sanders, or stationary and portable belt sanders. Coarse to fine papers are used in the beginning.

Final finishing is best done by hand rubbing with a fine powder, such as rottenstone mixed with linseed oil. Your choice of abrasives will affect the outcome of your handcrafted piece. Here are four points to keep in mind when finishing the wood:

1) Use the correct grade of sandpaper for the job. Mesh sizes range from 16 (the coarsest) to 600 (the finest).

2) Use the correct abrasive in conjunction with steel wool, sandpaper, or a rubbing cloth. Rottenstone is similar to talc, but is coarser and is to be used for very fine polishing. Silicon carbide is the hardest of the abrasive materials and should be used for rough sanding.

3) Sand with direction of the grain. Cross-grain sanding scratches rather than polishes the wood.

4) If steel wool is used for finishing, use the 0000 grade to obtain comparatively smooth surfaces.

A more detailed account of how to finish the wooden toy is found in the finishing section of this book and should be consulted for further information.

Some Helpful Hints Before You Begin

Every woodworker has his own style and his own favorite techniques and tricks. The following are some ideas and suggestions that I have devised or adopted and found useful in one or more of the projects discussed here.

• If you are inexperienced in woodworking techniques, use the butt joint to join two pieces of wood.

• The important thing to remember about the construction of a butt joint is that one must be accurate in sawing the right angles of the stock. An uneven cut will compound the worker's difficulty and render the joint weak, if not useless. Small gaps can easily be filled with commercial or homemade wood filler and then sanded afterward when the filler has hardened sufficiently to be worked.

• Wheels for toys are cut from dowels. Dowel rods are available in many lengths and diameters. The

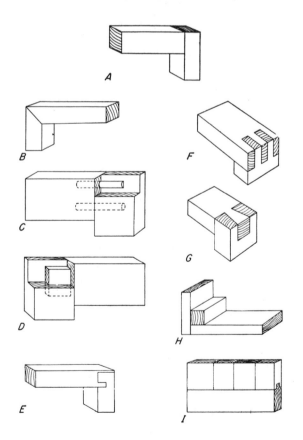

Figure III–1.
Methods of joining wood.
End-to-end grain joints: *A). End butt. B). Plane scarf. C). Serrated scarf. D). Finger. E). Onsrud. F). Hooked scarf. G). Double-slope scarf.*

End-to-side grain joints: *A). Butt. B). Miter. C). Dowel. D). Mortise and tenon. E). Dado tongue and rabbet. F). Slip or lock corner. G). Dovetail. H). Blocked. I). Tongue and groove.*

standard diameter sizes are 1/8 to 2 ½ inch. An old rolling pin will suffice for larger diameters. Chair and bench legs from discarded furniture or scraps from a woodturner's lathe bin might also prove useful.

• The actual cutting of the dowel should be done with a small toothed saw, such as a back saw. A too coarse blade will rip the fibers and splinter the edge. This necessitates sanding, which can invariably put the dowel "out of round." Use tape around the dowel to mark the cutting edge. This will also serve to minimize possible splintering as you saw.

• If an axle is to be centered through a wheel, mark the wheel at its exact center or else the wheel will become wobbly as the toy moves on the hard surface.

• Predrill intended screw holes with a drill bit smaller in diameter than the screw. It is also helpful to apply thick paste wax in very small amounts to the threaded portion of the screw. This lubricates the screw and wood as drilling is underway.

• Never discard wood scraps no matter what the size or condition. They may be used in future toys if only for accent pieces requiring minute amounts.

• Read manufacturer's instructions on all materials requiring mixing, application, and gluing. These directions, no matter how tedious, are designed to give their product optimal performance.

• If children are to play with the toys, use nontoxic materials to prevent accidental poisoning if parts are placed in the child's mouth or a splinter breaks the skin.

• Dust particles are the enemy of woodfinishers. As dust-free an environment as possible is the best one.

• Clean all brushes and articles that have come into contact with sealers, varnishes, stains, glues, paint, resins, and other material likely to soil or ruin reusable items. Consider the use of disposable materials such as very cheap hog bristle brushes, cardboard pails, plastic floor covers, dust mask filters, plastic aprons, and paper cups. Avoid styrofoam materials, as they are not resistant to most solvents.

• Mark all containers with contents, date of preparation, ingredients, "toxic" or "nontoxic," date of last use.

• Save small glass and metal jars to be used for storage of nails, pins, screws, brads, grommets, hinges, clips, touch-up brushes, washers, wing nuts, brads, staples, and a hundred other small items that are easily misplaced and that tend to clutter the workbench.

• If available, consider using a portable hair blower equipped with a heater switch. Today, this item is very cheap and can be used to dry small and hard to reach areas. It is not, however, recommended that the dryer be used for overall drying of glues, varnishes, etc, since these require slow, even drying for proper curing.

• If the wood is to be finished with lacquers or varnishes, try to suspend the item from an overhead wire by means of a hanger (coat hanger, thick wire). Air circulation all around the toy and as little contact with other objects as possible will facilitate the hardening of the finish.

• At the end of each work session, discard waste, exhausted pieces of sandpaper, steel wool, wood shavings, fragments of useless material, mixing containers, etc. Nothing is more depressing than having to return to the workbench the next day and face the leftovers of a woodman's orgy.

• Innocuous as they are, gnats, flies, ants, termites, and other tiny insects always seem to appear just as the can of varnish is opened and applied. I offset this nuisance by using an exhaust fan, which keeps insects at bay.

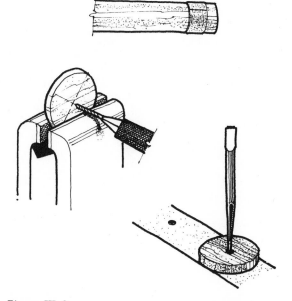

Figure III-2.
Dowels are best handled in the following manner: Top: Mark dowels by wrapping a small piece of masking tape around the dowel to act as a guide when sawing. Middle: To drill a hole through the center of a dowel disc, first clamp the disc in a vise and proceed to mark the center of the dowel. Drill the hole with a hand or power drill. Bottom: Use a center punch to dent the center of the disc when marking dowels to be used for wheels.

Tic-Tac-Toe (or Noughts and Squares)

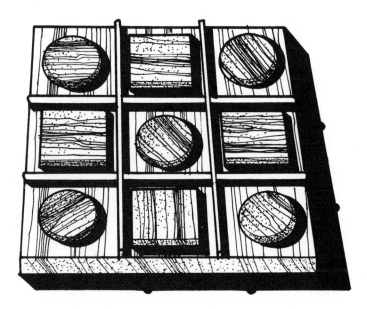

Figure III–3.
Tic-Tac-Toe (or Noughts and Squares).

A three-dimensional lap version of the age-old pencil game.

TOOLS
Coping saw
Crosscut handsaw
Keyhole saw
Coping saw
Drill
1/4-inch drill bit
C-clamps
T square
Ruler
Pencil and paper

MATERIALS
Wood
   (Use 3 to 4 different hardwoods. Cut circles from a dowel rod.)
   Base: (1) 12 by 12 inches
   Divisions: (2) ¼ by ½ by 12 inches
                (6) ¼ by ½ by 4 inches
   Circles: (5) 3 inches in diameter by ½ inch
   Squares: (5) 3 inches in diameter by ½ inch thick
Sandpaper, medium and fine grades
Steel wool, medium and fine grades
Glue
Masking tape
Leather pouch and drawstring (optional)
Finishing materials (*See instructions.*)

THE TOY
This is a relatively easy toy to make, and, when interesting woods are used, it makes a handsome contribution to the recreation area of the home. Place it on a low table and observe how many guests immediately engage themselves in the game. Sturdily built, it will withstand years of rigorous play. It is also an ideal pastime for long trips. It can be placed on a lap; each piece is confined to its own particular square, so it won't move around with the motion of the vehicle. Children love to put their hands on this one.

PROCEDURE
Use a flat piece of 12-inch-wide lumber that is absolutely square for the base. A T square and pencil will simplify the measuring and marking. Divide the base into nine equal squares, each measuring 4 by 4 inches. Now, you will notice in the illustration that the divisions are notched, enabling them to be inserted into the penciled grooves of the base. These grooves must be cut using the drill, bit, and coping saw. Drill holes to start the channel ¼ inch from the outer edge of the base. The two long divisions require an 11½-inch-long channel along two parallel penciled lines. The channels will also have to be divided into three equal lengths to accommodate the shorter divisions that are to be placed at right angles. Note that both ends of all the dividing strips of wood are notched. There are no exceptions.

The depths of the notches are measured and cut to either come up flush with the edge of the base or to overlap another division by half of its dividing strip's thickness.

Insert all divisions into the base after the base and strips have been sanded with sandpaper and steel wool to achieve a smooth surface. (Use medium and fine grades of sandpaper and steel wool.) Apply a conservative amount of glue to each piece and clamp in place. Allow sufficient time to dry. This is a good time to begin cutting the circles and squares.

The circles and squares are of identical diameter and thickness. They should be as true to their geometric shapes as possible. Mark one end of the dowel by means of masking tape. Saw slowly with a small-toothed blade, such as a crosscut hand saw or a coping saw. Sand each piece until it is smooth to the touch starting with coarse and working to fine sandpaper.

Each player has a maximum of five circles or squares with which to play. A good way to accent the different shapes is to use a light-colored wood (ash, beech, oak) for one shape and a dark-colored wood (black walnut, ebony, teak) for the other.

FINISHING

Apply wax of the paste variety, such as carnauba or trewax, and rub until both base and parts are brought to a lustrous finish. If you intend to use a sealer, such as lacquer or polyurethane, either brush or spray the sealer in quick, even passes with the brush or can. Blot any residue that may build up on the edges and sides of the work.

If desired, a few passes with 0000 steel wool will level out the high spots of the sealer. Too much rubbing with steel wool, however, tends to dull the finish and can actually drive small strands of the wool into the finish, and these are not easily removed.

An extra touch for storage of the squares and circles is a handmade leather pouch with a drawstring. The leather serves to buff the woods and over the years will give them a pleasing patina.

If you wish to raise the playing board off the table, cut four pieces of the leftover dowel to ¼-inch lengths and glue on the underside of the base at each corner.

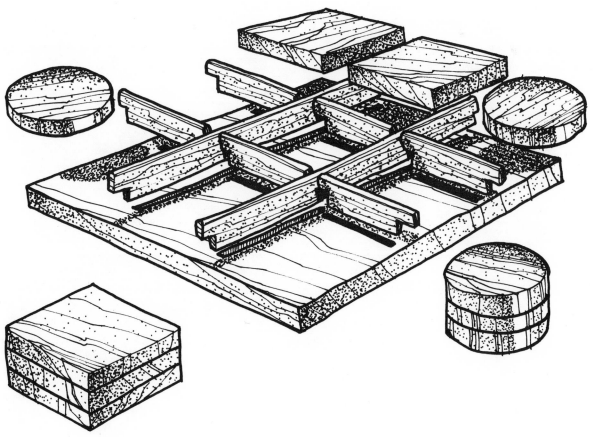

Figure III–4.
Exploded view of the board and pieces.

Flatbed Lorry

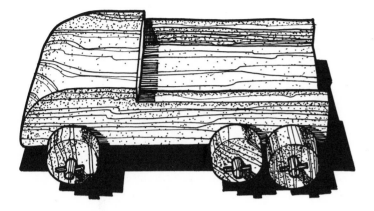

Figure III–5.
Flatbed Lorry.

A low-profile truck with an airflow design meant for hauling heavy-duty goods.

TOOLS
Handsaw
Coping saw
Drill
1/8-inch drill bit
3/8-inch drill bit
Ruler or T square
Rasp
C-clamps
Center punch
Pencil and paper

MATERIALS
Wood
    (Use an oak wood block for the main piece and a dark hardwood for the sides. Cut wheels, axles, and cotter pins from dowel rods.)
    Main piece: (1) 4 by 4 by 10 inches
    Railing sides: (2) 2 by ½ by 7 inches
    Wheels: (6) 2 inches in diameter, thickness is optional
    Axles: (3) 3/8 inch in diameter by 7 inches
    Cotter pins: (6) 1/8 inch in diameter by 1 inch
Glue
Sandpaper, coarse, medium, and fine grades
2 small brass brads (optional)
Finishing materials (*See instructions.*)

THE TOY
Trucks have long been immensely appealing to children and adults alike. Their functional, streamlined design belies their brute strength, which makes them all the more awesome-looking as they perform their Herculean tasks. The design for this particular truck is derived from the aerodynamic design of cars and airplanes from the 1930s and early 40s. The windswept fenders and cab, devoid of tacky and protruding hardware, gave them the look and style of the future's technology. This version becomes symbolic of all trucks because it has a decidedly "no-nonsense" contour.

This is a hefty toy, and underneath its simple exterior should lie good craftsmanship. Dimensions of the wood may be modified to either enlarge or reduce the overall size. Grain marks in the woods, as well as contrasting colors, will make this a very special project, which can be built with an economy of time and material.

PROCEDURE
Use woods that you have carefully examined for color and grain striations. Think in terms of placement of the parts and the smooth, well-rounded wheels. All surface contours should be of continuous flow; i.e., flat and at right angles where needed. The cab should also reveal a natural curve free of bumps and dents.

Cut the wood block as specified and draw measurements on both its broad surfaces. Draw an outline on the narrow edge with a ruler or T square. Saw all the individual wood parts away from each other and shape them according to your specified dimensions. Begin with lengthwise saw cuts wherever possible, then saw crosswise and diagonally.

Round off the cab with the coping saw, then further smooth the surface with coarse sandpaper or a rasp. File and sand with the grain to prevent the wood from breaking up.

Drill three holes through the block with the 3/8-inch drill bit and insert the matching dowels so that they protrude from both sides an equal amount. (The axles are not meant to spin. The rolling motion will be accomplished by the wheels turning freely on the axle. If the wood wheels tend to bind on the chassis, insert a piece of thin leather to act as a bushing.) Drill through the center of each wheel and place them in position on the axles. Drill the ends of the axle in the center with the 1/8-inch bit. It is a good idea to place the dowel wheels in a vise or to clamp them to a scrap piece of wood while drilling. If the wheels are not anchored, they tend to spin when the drill bit engages the wood. Also, by tapping a slight indentation with a center punch, the drill bit is less likely to be deflected from its path. Insert small dowel strips to act as ''cotter pins,'' which will prevent the wheels from coming off.

Glue the two railing sides to the bottom and edge surfaces with a small amount of glue. Clamp and let stand until thoroughly dry.

An optional addition to the front of the truck would be two small brass brads. These would represent headlights and would nicely complement the oak.

FINISHING

Because of its hardness, oak must be worked slowly with sandpaper and steel wool. Sand with the grain in short strokes, applying more or less pressure where needed to remove crosscut marks. If the wheels do not spin freely, and, once you have determined that the hole in the wheel is not too small, add a small amount of paste wax to both the inside of the wheel and the axle tips. The cotter-pin dowels are to be permanent and are made so with a couple of drops of wood glue.

Apply the finish only after the wood has been rubbed with a piece of cheesecloth to remove all dirt and dust particles. Either paste wax or an oil finish prepared from one of the recipes given *(see finishes)* will do nicely. A clear sealer, as an alternative, will give the wood a more permanent finish by closing up the pores.

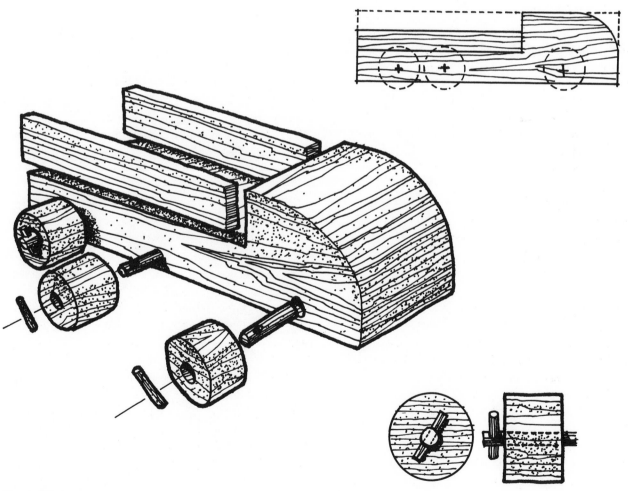

Figure III–6.
Exploded view of the truck. The upper right illustration shows the shape of the toy in relation to the original block of wood.

Dump the Hat

Figure III–7.
Dump the Hat.

A game requiring skill and accuracy with marbles.

TOOLS
Coping saw
Handsaw
Drill
¼-inch drill bit
3/8-inch drill bit
Center punch
Indelible marking pen
Ruler
Pencil, paper, and carbon paper

MATERIALS
Wood
  (Use light hardwood for the bodies and dark hardwood for the 2 bases and stands.)
  Heads: (4) round knobs
  Hats: (4) large wood buttons
      (Circles from a dowel may be substituted.)
  Bodies: (4) ½ by 1½ by 5 inches
  Bases: (2) ½ by 1 by 5 inches
  Stands: (2) ½ by 1¾ by 6 inches
  Caps: (2) ½ inch in diameter by ½ inch
      (Cut from a dowel.)
Dowel, ¼ inch in diameter by 27 inches
Glass agate or wood marbles
Glue
Finishing materials (See instructions.)

THE TOY
This is a toy that dates back to the Orient of the 1700s where the game was played as a modified version of the Greek and Roman game of skittles. In this version the figures spin on a dowel rod. The objective is to pitch a marble along the ground, aiming it at the base of one of the standing figures. If the pitch is accurate and strikes the base, the figure swings up and the wood hat is doffed onto the floor. The person who racks up the highest number of hats is the winner.

The game can be made to encompass as many figures as you wish simply by using a longer strip of dowel. This is particularly desirable when there are likely to be more than two players at one time. To make things even more interesting zones with various scores can be ruled out on paper and placed in front of the stand. When the hat lands in a scoring zone, the points are added up. Whoever tallies the most, wins.

There is a wide variety of unusual wood buttons available in yardage stores, so consider buying several for the hats on the wooden gentlemen. The buttons are often decorative and handsomely turned. Many of these buttons lend themselves to staining or just plain polishing. Whatever you decide, be sure to keep an abundance of marbles available, as they are often lost; the game becomes quite heated and the marbles fly along the ground like miniature bowling balls, winging their way toward the wooden pins.

PROCEDURE
On paper draw the outline of the model figure. The body tapers toward the bottom so that misdirected marbles will be able to pass through. Decide on the number of figures your toy will have and transfer the drawing to the pieces of wood by means of carbon paper. Cut out the figures with the coping saw. Locate the center of the top edge in each figure and drill a hole to a depth of about 3/8 inch. Insert a 1¾-inch length of ¼-inch dowel into each hole, having applied a small amount of glue to the tips of each. Allow to dry.

Drill holes through the shoulder edge of the figures (both sides) and string them onto an 18-inch dowel. In between each figure, a small wood marble or ball is placed to keep the figures from sliding to the left or right. (Very small drawer pulls found in hardware stores can be used for this purpose.) The figures must spin freely. Give them a preliminary flick or two with your finger to be assured they will spin without binding.

Note that the dowel must extend beyond the two outermost figures by at least 1¼ inch. This will permit the ends to pass through the two vertical stands that support the figures.

Drill a hole through each round knob and button with the ¼-inch bit. Once the dowels in the top edge of the figure have dried, place the round knobs (which represent the heads) on the protruding dowel. Glue in place. Slip the wood buttons over the remaining tips and see if they readily fall off as the figure pitches forward or backward. It may be necessary to enlarge the hole in the button to make it fit loosely.

The size of the two bases is determined by the overall size of the toy. The larger the toy, the more substantial the bases must be. A hefty marble, given a good, experienced flick could topple the toy or force one end to move away from a position parallel to the viewer. For example, if the figures number six in all, measure approximately 5 inches in height, and are thin (3/8 inch), then the two end bases should measure ½ by 2 by 4 inches and the vertical posts, ½ by ½ by 5½ inches. This will provide the necessary weight to keep the toy steady, but will not be so large as to become unmanageable. After you have cut the bases to size, glue a vertical post to each base. These vertical supports should be approximately the height of the figures plus ½ inch.

To position the horizontal dowel with figures on the stand, drill a hole in each vertical post, using a 3/8-inch bit. The holes should be placed high enough for the figures to swing freely and low enough so that the marbles can strike the figures. To hold the horizontal dowel in place, insert the ends through the holes in the vertical posts and butt-join the two ½-inch caps with glue.

Draw faces on the wood knobs with an indelible marking pen. The more experienced woodworker may wish to predrill and inlay small pieces of contrasting wood to create an expression of his own design. The inlay pieces are sanded smooth, flush to the surface of the knob. Some of my students have gone to great lengths in using interesting materials, such as colored gemstones, enameled trim, and even mother-of-pearl, to decorate the faces and bodies of the figures. The results reveal the marks of seasoned craftsmen.

To complement the assorted light and dark woods search for old marbles such as ''cat's-eye'' or swirled glass. These older marbles have a wonderfully aged look and feel, and, unfortunately, are no longer made in the same fashion as they were many years ago. Store the marbles in a matching wood box or leather pouch. The smaller the marble, the more difficult the game becomes.

FINISHING

A game of this type is likely to receive an inordinate amount of use, and the continued striking against the figures and other parts subjects them to real wear and tear. Finish this type of toy with a sealer, such as clear lacquer, which will not alter the color of the wood, but will provide a mar-proof finish that will enable the toy to withstand the rigors of play. Apply two to three coats of the lacquer, sanding with fine sandpaper between each coat. A final rubdown with steel wool will eliminate bubbles and other surface impurities and will give an even sheen to the woods.

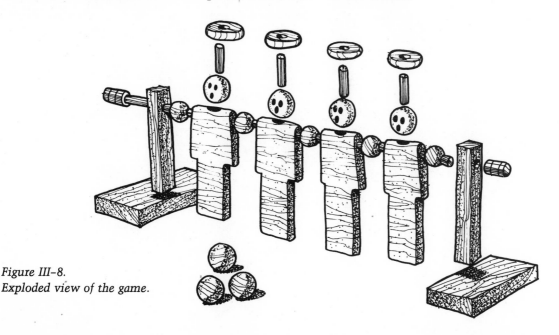

Figure III–8.
Exploded view of the game.

57

African Slit Drum

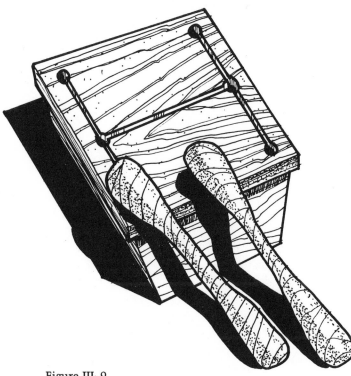

Figure III-9.
African Slit Drum.

A ceremonial bush instrument.

TOOLS
Handsaw
Keyhole saw
Drill
¼-inch drill bit
3/8-inch drill bit
Ruler
Wood putty and putty knife or round plug and
   mallet
Pencil and paper

MATERIALS
Wood
   (Use mahogany or teak.)
   Top: (1) 1 by 8 by 12 inches
   Long sides: (2) 1 by 6 by 12 inches
   Short sides: (2) 1 by 6 by 8 inches
   Bottom: (1) 1 by 8 by 12 inches
2 dowels, 1 inch in diameter by 10 inches (To be
wrapped with a long strip of fabric, such as cotton or
sailcloth; if leather is preferred, long strips of boot
rawhide can be used.)
16 flat-head wood screws, 1 inch long
Carpenter's hide glue
Finishing materials (*See instructions.*)

THE INSTRUMENT
The African slit drum is used in ceremonies and for
telegraphing messages through the bush. Traditionally, the slit drum is made by laboriously
hollowing out the log through a slit along its length.
One end may be given a wide bore, producing a deep
"male" note; narrow bores give lighter tones.

The wood is chosen for its durability. In some
cultures drum making is performed in association
with solemn rituals to enlist the cooperation of the
wood itself and the spirit world. It is believed that
the tree must be felled at the auspicious moment
and dropped in the auspicious direction. In some
African cultures it is believed that water, a spirit in
its own way, must be avoided by the drum maker
while the drum fabrication is under way. In the
Solomon Islands it is believed that long ago the
ocean arose from a slit drum. Mystic connections
between the drum and the wood have long
permeated the practice of drum making. For the
contemporary woodworker there is a profound
sense of folklore, as well as sheer skill, involved in
the craft.

The drumsticks must be shrouded with enough
material to produce a "thud" as they strike the top
surface. This covering also prevents the denting of
the wood. The drumstick taps the top of the wood
at any chosen point. Each area of the surface gives a
high or low sound, depending on the proximity of
the taps to the slits. The overall configuration of the
drum may be enlarged to produce a deeper sound. A
drum made of smaller dimensions will not provide
the necessary depth of sound or bass notes.

PROCEDURE

All pieces of wood should be cut to the above dimensions. If a rectangular drum suits your design, you may want to just butt-join all pieces of wood for the sake of simplicity. However, a mitered edge on all pieces marked for joining will provide a better-looking project. If you use the miter method, increase the size of the lumber by 1 inch for each mitered edge. Consider tapering the sides of the drum so that the base is narrower than the top, much like a conga drum. This will appreciably alter the sound. In any event, experiment with several shapes to find the ones most pleasing.

The top piece is to be predrilled to accept the wood screws. The longer sides are to have three equidistant holes drilled. The side pieces will go beneath the top, directly below the holes. The short sides of the top of the drum need only be bored with two holes, one hole in the middle of each side. The holes on the longer side will be joined by cut slits between them, as pictured in the illustration. Best results are obtained when the slits are at least 1½ inches from the edges of the box. The lines do not necessarily have to parallel one another. If the two opposing slits gradually incline toward each other, but do not actually converge or intersect, then it is at this end of the instrument that a higher note can be sounded.

The side pieces are glued to the top with a butt or mitered joint and allowed to set up. The top is then fastened to the top, and the bottom is attached in the same manner.

All flat-head screws are countersunk. This is done by drilling with a larger drill bit into the existing hole, just deep enough to seat the head below the wood's surface. Even for the inexperienced woodworker, this should pose no problem. Some experimentation on a scrap of wood will give you the feel of how deep to drill.

Filling the small remaining hole is done in one of two ways. The first and simplest method is to apply wood putty to the surface, forcing the filler into the hole with the finger. The glue, which is the binder for the filler, sets up within minutes, and, therefore, it must be worked quickly. As the filler begins to harden but remains pliable, gently remove all excess filler using a stiff-edged tool, such as a putty knife, cardboard edge, plastic scraper, etc. What remains is to be flush with the surface of the wood. Choose a filler that closely matches the wood's color or one that is extremely light by contrast for a "pegged" effect.

The second option is more tricky, but is professional in appearance and is practiced by most craftsmen. This is known as "plugging the hole" and is done by means of a round plug, usually a small piece of dowel, which can be stained to match the wood or left its natural color to accent. The diameter of the plug is to be just slightly larger than the diameter of the drill used to bore the hole in the wood. A ½-inch bore made by the respective drill bit does not always permit a snug fit for the corresponding dowel. Because of the angle of the cut, inaccurate milling of the dowel, wood expansion, and a host of other intangibles, it is important to be prepared for some slight adjustments as the holes are pegged. The plug is, in essence, a cap. It is to be driven into the hole by means of a soft-faced mallet. (A hard hammer would be likely to flare the top of the dowel and might possibly split the whole thing.) A bad plug is easily removed by drilling out the waste with a drill and bit. Any parts remaining above the surface can be lightly sanded to be made smooth.

The drums that sound the best are those made with a proper, tight seating and joining of all edges. Cracks can be filled on both sides before the top is finally positioned and screwed down. File or plane all edges that extend beyond the corner of the drum.

The drumsticks are carefully and tightly wound with the suggested materials. This is not an involved operation. Note that both ends of the drumsticks are larger than the center shaft. This is done because double wrapping of fabric or leather gives a softer head to both ends. When used to strike the drum, the soft end helps to produce a more mellow sound than a lightly wrapped stick. Cotton filler may be used in place of the double wrap.

FINISHING

An instrument of this type is best finished by means of traditional sanding with medium to fine sandpaper, followed by steel wool and staining. Staining can be very effective when applied to mahogany, teak, or any other wood for that matter. Use a stain that doesn't mask the natural properties of the wood, but simply makes it appear richer by slightly darkening the existing, innate color. After staining, wax or oil, such as lemon oil (a yellowish substance), can be briskly rubbed into the wood. The disadvantage here is that the wax or oil only remains in the grain for a short time. Oil becomes tacky to the touch in a matter of weeks, if it is not thoroughly rubbed with a cheesecloth to occasionally remove the residue it develops. On the other hand, oil, which penetrates the wood, brings about a rich luster and a pronounced sheen, unlike wax, which is only superficial.

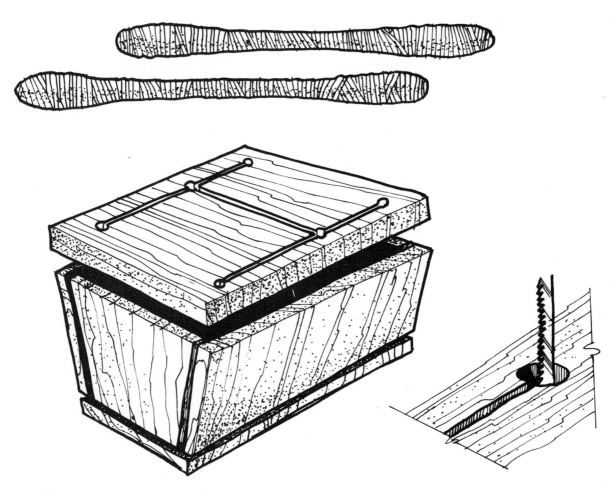

Figure III–10.
Exploded view of the drum and illustration of the saw blade passing through predrilled hole for slit-cutting process.

Train Puzzle

Figure III–11.
Train Puzzle.

A puzzle of low relief made of hardwoods with pronounced grain.

TOOLS
Handsaw
Coping saw
Hand drill
¼-inch drill bit
Clamps
Ruler
Graph paper
Carbon paper
Pencil and paper

MATERIALS
Wood
  (Use mixed hardwoods, such as zebrawood, padouk, and walnut.)
  Top and Base Planks: (12 to 15) ¼ inch by assorted widths by 20 inches
  Wheels: (6) wood discs, 1½ inches in diameter by ½ inch
  Tracery: 1 strip of light hardwood, ¼ by ¼ inch by 4 feet
Glue
Finishing materials *(See instructions.)*

THE TOY
Here is a puzzle that is practically more fun to build than it is to use. It is composed of a variety of hardwoods of thin widths—a good way to put many of your leftover scraps to use. The illustrated version was made of zebrawood, padouk, ponderosa pine, and walnut. The train's wheels are glued to the surface of the board, rather than being inset; the locomotive and cars are inset. The real job here is to laminate as much wood as you can and then, by means of a drill and coping saw, cut out the negative shapes that comprise the train.

PROCEDURE
Draw the shape of the train on graph paper. Glue the long edges of the 20-inch strips together, so that they are laminated edge-to-edge, and clamp until dry. Cut the dried laminated wood in half to make two 10-inch-long planks. One plank serves as the base, the other will have the positive forms cut free from the inside and will then be glued on top of the base.

Transfer the drawing to the top plank. Drill holes in the corners of each train car to begin cutting with the coping saw. There are three shapes cut from this plank, one for the engine and then the two cars. Apply the thin strips of light wood to form a tracery of pattern on the surface of each car as shown in the illustration. Glue, position, and clamp in place.

Apply wheel discs to the surface of the top plank and let dry. These may be placed at any interval. Glue the top plank to the bottom plank and clamp. Sand all surfaces with medium and fine sandpaper. This is especially crucial to the outer edges of the puzzle parts to ensure an easy fit.

FINISHING
Woods of this variety have the best appearance and feel when they are finished without stains, lacquers, or other chemical sealing agents. To give a hand-rubbed finish, apply a generous coat of carnauba paste wax to the surface and let stand for one hour. Buff the surface with a cloth. Then repeat the process without the hour's wait. Several repeats will bring the wood to a velvety finish, giving it an even richer look.

Gravity-Defying Ball Box

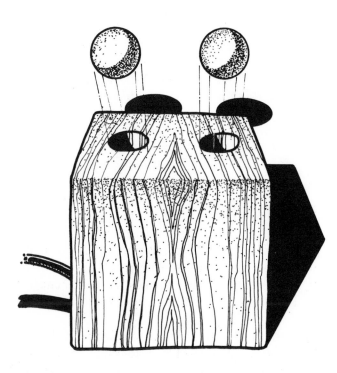

Figure III-12.
Gravity-Defying Ball Box.

A toy that creates the illusion of balls floating in midair with no visible means of attachment or support.

TOOLS

Crosscut handsaw or radial-arm saw
Adjustable power saw or table saw
Drill
¼-inch drill bit
1-inch auger bit and brace
Wood clamps
Half-round keyhole file
Screwdriver
Pliers
Ruler
Compass
Pencil and paper

MATERIALS

Wood
(Use hardwood such as elm, pear wood, purpleheart, or brown oak. Brazilian rosewood would make this a very handsome contribution to the interior of your home.)
Top: (1) ½ by 12 by 12 inches
Bottom: (1) ½ by 12 by 12 inches
Sides: (4) ½ by 11 by 11 inches

1 piece of common wood, 1 by 12 by 12 inches

Small electric fan (the type used to keep small appliances and machinery cool. They generate less than ¼ horsepower and are available from electrical-supply sources or small-appliance repair stores.)

Glue

2 Ping-Pong balls

Zip cord with male plug

2 bolts, 1½ inch, 1/8 inch in diameter, and matching nuts

Finishing materials (*See instructions.*)

THE TOY

Every student of physics has observed this phenomenon: Strong air current can be directed through a small opening (much like the exhaust end of a vacuum cleaner), sustained by means of a motor equipped with a fan, and used to keep two lightweight objects (in this case Ping-Pong balls) afloat for an indefinite period of time. When the motor is hidden inside of a richly grained, mysterious box, the phenomenon becomes more enigmatic. Once the motor is turned on and the two balls put in place, they appear to float with no visible means of support. The thick wood absorbs much of the whirring sound, so it's anyone's guess as to how this feat is accomplished.

As this project involves the flow of electric current, it is essential that current and motor be compatible. Ask an electrician if in doubt.

PROCEDURE

By means of a crosscut handsaw or radial-arm saw, cut out all premeasured pieces of hardwood to make a six-sided box of equal dimensions. The box should be constructed by using a mitered edge technique throughout. This usually involves the use of an adjustable power saw or table saw capable of cutting miters on stock more than 3 inches in height. If you are not equipped to make this type of cut, then use the butt-joint method, which works just as well, but lacks the finished look of mitered joints.

The top piece is measured for the two holes, which are to be bored with the brace and auger bit. The placement and diameter of each hole is critical. Therefore, divide the top in half with a pencil and ruler and find the exact center of the rectangular space you have ruled out. Proceed to bore the holes at the center marks of the left and right side of the top. Finish the inside of the hole by filing with the half-round file until the wall is smooth to the touch. The top is momentarily set aside, and the rest of the box should be assembled at this point.

With bolts and nuts, mount the small exhaust fan on a piece of wood that has been precut to fit the inside of the box, making sure that it is a tight fit. (The slight and continued vibration of the motor might otherwise dislodge the base of the motor.) Place the motor and its attached base inside the box and secure there by means of glue or by mounting the entire assembly on two strips of wood that have previously been glued to the insides of the box. The topmost part of the motor should be no less than 1 inch from the underside of the top lid.

Drill a hole in the back panel at the bottom of the box to allow for the insertion of the power cord (with plug attachment removed). Once the cord has been threaded, attach the plug. Position the top panel by means of glue or flat-head wood screws, which will enable you to remove the lid if the motor fails. In any event, always test the toy before the top is permanently affixed to make sure that no further adjustments are necessary and that it does indeed work.

FINISHING

There are several possible ways to finish the gravity-defying ball box.

All hardwoods require a good and thorough sanding with the grain to remove saw marks and scratches. Consider following up with fine emery paper or Carborundum paper. Apply paste wax and rub with cheesecloth. Switch to a terry cloth fabric or an old bath towel (to be used for its nap) to further highlight the finish. Polyurethane or varathane may also be used to seal the wood and give your toy a low sheen or satin finish.

Figure III–13.
Interior view of Gravity-Defying Ball Box showing fan mechanism and its placement in regard to Ping-Pong ball.

Zebrawood Yo-Yo

Figure III–14.
Zebrawood Yo-Yo.

An elegant and unique adaptation of one of the world's oldest toys.

TOOLS

If your workshop is equipped with a wood lathe and wood-turning gouges and chisels, this is an ideal project for you, the more professionally equipped craftsman. Although wood-turning is not taught in this book, there are many books that you may want to consult, if you need further instruction in the correct operation of these tools (see *Wood Turning*, by Stephen Hogbin, published by Van Nostrand Reinhold). For the less professionally equipped woodworker, the following tools will be needed:

Handsaw
Coping saw
Drill
3/8-inch drill bit
C-clamps
Surform tool or wood rasp
Mallet
Wood gouges
Chisels
Nail punch
Pencil and paper

MATERIALS

Wood
  (Use zebrawood.)
  1 piece of wood, ½ (or 1) by 6 inches by 2 feet
Dowel, 3/8 inch in diameter by 1¼ inches
Glue
Braided string
Finishing materials (*See instructions.*)

THE TOY

The yo-yo is a toy of extraordinary universality. Throughout history, the yo-yo has emerged again and again in cultures throughout the world who could not possibly have been in touch with one another at those times. Sometimes the toy vanished for centuries only to appear in some remote area with no apparent predecessor.

The yo-yo was known in the ancient Far East and was used as a weapon in the Philippines. A soldier would hide in a tree or dense grass and strike his victim with a fatal blow. During the 1920s in both England and America, the yo-yo swept the land and became a favorite plaything of grown-ups and children alike. The impact was so pronounced that it caused a Persian newspaper journalist to write the following angry protest, which denounced the toy for its immoral and dangerous potential:

> . . . this game, like the deadly plagues which used to come from India or Arabia, has come from Europe . . . even mothers who formerly attended to the care of children and households, now spend all their time playing yo-yo.

Obviously, the yo-yo never quite kept·pace with this ominous account. It has since become one of the standard and best-loved toys in the world.

PROCEDURE

On a piece of cardboard draw a circle of the diameter you want. To keep the toy manageable and practical do not exceed 5 inches. Draw another circle on a separate sheet of cardboard slightly smaller than the first circle. Transfer the circles, two of each size, to the wood. With the handsaw, cut the wood into four pieces, one for each circle. Each circle (two small ones and two large ones) is cut from the board with the coping saw. The cut must be accurate; proceed slowly to minimize the chance of cutting the wood "out of round."

Once all four circles have been cut, prepare to glue and C-clamp a small circle to a larger circle.

(This represents one-half of the finished form. It makes no difference which half is right or left.) Repeat this step for the other two pieces. Apply a thin layer of glue to the surfaces that are to be contacted, making sure the smaller circle is centered on the larger one. Apply and tighten the clamps.

When the laminated sections have fully cured, remove the clamps and place one section on the worktable. Clamp in place. To achieve a beveled edge on the smaller circle, use chisels, gouges, and a light touch with your mallet to shape the desired angle around the circle. This results in a rough surface, which is then made smooth by short strokes with a wood rasp or Surform rasp. The illustration shows but one person's version of effective lamination and angle refinement. Yours may be made rounder or squarer. Repeat this technique with the other half, making sure both halves are balanced in weight and form.

Locate and mark the centers of the insides of the larger circles with a pencil or nail punch. Holes are drilled in both to a depth of ½ inch. Apply glue to both ends of the short dowel and insert each end into its respective hole by applying pressure to both sides of the yo-yo. Both halves of the yo-yo are to be parallel; if askew, the toy will not spin properly and this slows down the momentum.

Select a good piece of braided string and wax it slightly to retard fraying. A slip knot is made in loop fashion and slipped over the halves. Pull the string tight. Spin the yo-yo to see if the axle turns freely within the slip knot. If it binds, apply a small amount of wax by means of a thin brush to the axle.

FINISHING

Zebrawood is absolutely beautiful when wax and wax alone is used after extensive sanding with 0000 steel wool. Use the carnauba wax, which is free of synthetic agents and abrasives. The more rubbing you can manage, the more glossy the finish will be. And don't get in the path of "loop the loop" or "around the world" with this creation. This is a beefy yo-yo that requires real strength and stamina to perform the standard repertoire of tricks and moves. Duncan and Champion . . . move over.

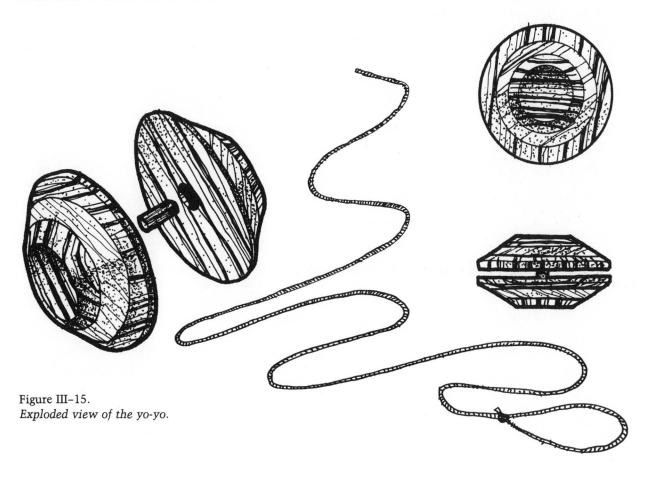

Figure III–15.
Exploded view of the yo-yo.

Tumble Box

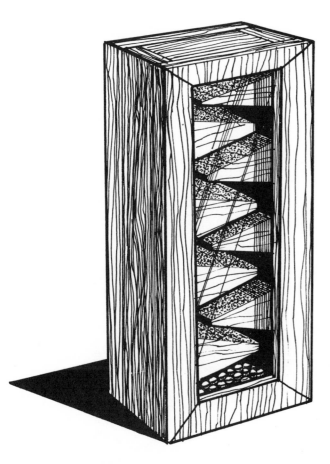

Figure III–16.
Tumble Box.

Ball bearings cascade down a series of shelves to produce a sustained tapping sound. Turn the box upside down and do it again.

TOOLS

Handsaw
Backsaw
Hand drill
¼-inch drill bit
3/8-inch drill bit
Miter box (optional)
Adjustable wood clamp
Screwdriver
Ruler or T square
Pencil and paper

MATERIALS

Wood
(Use walnut or any hardwood. Woods may be mixed or matched; i.e., dark woods: cherry, elm, or hickory, and light woods: maple, sugar pine, or yellow cedar. Cut wedges from a rectangular block.)
Window frames sides: (4) 1 by 1 by 16 inches
Window frames tops and bottoms: (4) 1 by 1 by 7 inches
Box sides: (2) 1 by 5 by 16 inches
Box top and bottom: (2) 1 by 5 by 5 inches
Wedges: (8) 1 by 3 by 5
2 sheets of clear acrylic plastic, 3/16 by 7 by 16 inches
30 small ball bearings (pea size)
Glue (one that will adhere wood and plastic)
Wood screws (optional)
Finishing materials (*See instructions.*)

THE TOY

The tumble box provides an endless amount of enjoyment accompanied by an almost continuous clattering sound as the bearings slowly wend their way from one shelf to the other. Made well, it is practically indestructible. The Plexiglas (acrylic) sheets allow the player to observe the bearings as they roll from the top to their resting place at the bottom of the maze.

Variations of size can be attempted; the taller the box, the longer the ride down. The shelves must be cut to allow free travel of the bearings. This way, few, if any, will become temporarily disrupted in motion.

Provided that a good-quality wood glue is used on all parts requiring glued assembly, no nails or screws are necessary for this project.

PROCEDURE

Mark measurements on the narrow edge of the wood and all surfaces where cutting lines are to be followed. Use a T square or ruler for right-angle drawing. Carry measurements over to the broad surface. Then saw out the individual pieces. The grain in all pieces of wood should run in the same direction if possible.

Glue window frames first. Mitering with the miter box will do the job. Glue and clamp; wipe off excess glue.

The two side panels (these are to hold the wedges) are then placed flat on the worktable. A word first about the wedges: The wedge angle is not critical to the overall performance of the toy, but the less steep they are, the slower and more drawn out the movement of the bearings will be. To make the wedge mark the center point on the 3-inch side of the 3- by 5-inch block of wood. Draw a line from this point to each opposing corner and cut along the lines using a backsaw. Once the wedges are complete, the base of each wedge is positioned on the two panels. Make sure that all wedges are positioned evenly. Then glue and clamp and allow them to stand for the complete curing period.

Place all facets of the box, including the Plexiglas sheets, together. Apply glue to all the joining surfaces. Before installing the top, pour the ball bearings into the box and observe the falling motion for proper travel. If the balls bind, check to make sure that the wedges are properly aligned. They should appear to mesh but must in no way touch, as this would hamper the flow of the ball bearings.

If desired, to make a unified box, fasten the outer frame of both sides of the window to the outer frame, the Plexiglas, and the two side panels with wood screws.

Once the design has been checked out, secure the top panel with glue or wood screws. As in all instances when screws are used, they should be countersunk and their cavities filled with wood paste or filler.

FINISHING

If kerf marks or unsightly saw cuts are apparent, slowly sand the wood in the correct grain growth pattern. Abrasives, other than those designed for plastic, will spoil the surface of the plastic; therefore, caution should be exercised when sanding.

A steel wool rubbing with a small dollop of paste wax into the surface of the wood is next. If sealer or lacquer is applied, all plastic surfaces should be masked, to prevent inadvertent splashes or droplets from coming into contact with them.

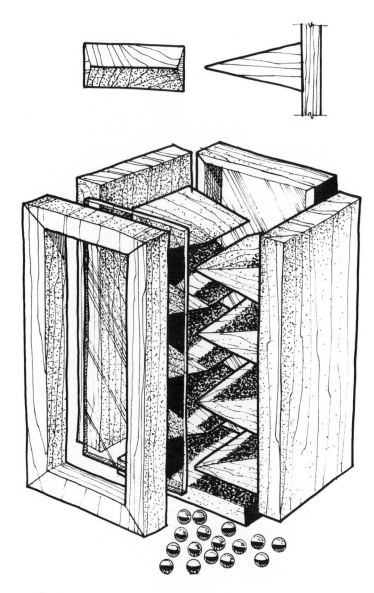

Figure III–17.
Exploded view of tumble box and detail of the wedge.

Three-Dimensional Jigsaw Puzzle and Case

Figure III–18.
Three-Dimensional Jigsaw Puzzle.

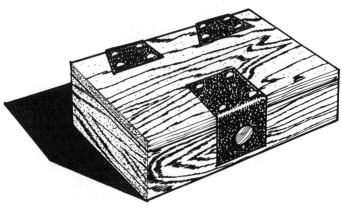

Figure III–19.
Case for puzzle.

A box of assorted hardwoods and softwoods of all colors housed in its own carrying case.

TOOLS
Handsaw
Coping saw
Backsaw
Adjustable wood clamps
Miter box
Hammer
Ruler
Graph paper
Pencil and paper

MATERIALS
Wood
(Use an assortment of many exotic and colorful woods. This is where all your good scraps come into good use. Select woods of contrasting color, texture, grain, growth pattern, and overall shape. You will need at least 9 pieces no smaller than 3 inches square.)
Sides, bottom, and top panels: ½-inch stock measured and cut to your specifications to accommodate your final arrangement of wood pieces. Example: 4 pieces, each 9 by 3 by ½ inch, for sides, and 2 pieces, each 9 by 9 by ½ inch for top and bottom.
1 wood cabinet knob and attaching screw and nut
2 pieces of leather for hinges, 2 by 3 inches
1 piece of leather for securing lid to frame, 3 by 5 inches
Carbon paper
Sandpaper, grades 120 and 220
Glue
Brass brads or brass round-head wood screws
Saddle soap or leather polish
Finishing materials (*See instructions.*)

THE TOY
Jigsaw puzzles, like crossword puzzles, are addictive. There is something inescapably challenging about putting the pieces back together the way they belong. However, in this version, there are no helpful pictures to steer you in the right direction. You must deduce the correct fit by guesswork based solely on fit and careful arrangement.

Smaller pieces with more intricate cuts make the puzzle all the more perplexing and can break even the most die-hard, inveterate puzzle solver.

PROCEDURE
With graph paper and pencil decide precisely how the pieces are to fit with one another.

One comment before you design the pattern for your puzzle: The stores are fraught with picturesque puzzles of the jigsaw variety. Keep your design abstract. The library is full of books on pattern zigzag motifs and a whole host of interesting free-form and geometric designs from all over the world. Islamic, Byzantine, Hopi Indian, Peruvian, and South Sea Island ornaments are among some of the richest stylizations available. Consult them for inspirations for your particular design. This becomes your working blueprint from which the cuts of the miscellaneous pieces of wood are to be made.

Transfer all drawings to the select pieces of wood, using carbon paper, and proceed to cut the wood remnants to conform to your blueprint. There should be no tight curves. Gentle arching angles make for a simpler fit and do not involve overly intricate tooling. Test the pieces as you go along, assuring proper seating and meshing where necessary.

Rough areas or pieces of wood with bumps should be block sanded or planed even. Although it is conceivable that you might want pieces of varying heights, the overall appearance is better if all pieces are kept to the same height.

The box, into which the parts of the puzzle are to be placed, follows the same lines as that of a cigar box; however, this one is larger.

Miter both ends of the four side boards to form right angles. Assemble, glue, and clamp with adjustable wood clamps the four sides of the box. Allow enough height in the sides to accommodate the inset base, which serves as both the bottom of the box and the puzzle base. Install the base with glue and allow to dry.

Cut the lid to cover the overall box, flush to all four sides. The top may be of one piece of wood or, for increased visual interest, a laminated board made with a variety of woods may be used.

After the project has been finished, carefully place the leather hinges toward the outer dimension of the lid. Cut the leather with sharp, smooth-bladed scissors. Fasten the leather in place with a hammer and a brad or brass round-head wood screw. Use as many as is necessary to keep the leather from curling or flapping. A supple leather will make opening and closing of the box easier and will wear well with age. A leather that is too thin may not hold up well and will need replacing soon. Once the two leather hinges have been attached, measure and cut the front leather strip, which will be used to latch the box. Note in the illustration that the leather has been cut to fit over the knob. Therefore, the size of the hole in the leather is determined by the dimensions of the knob. The leather used for the strip must be supple enough to stretch slightly over the knob but must recoil a bit to provide a snug fit. Fasten the leather in place on top of the lid with brass brads or with brass round-head wood screws, which will give you a more secure join. The leather may be treated with saddle soap or polish to keep it preserved and in supple condition.

FINISHING

A full assortment of stains and sealers are at your disposal. If your search for exotic woods has been fruitless, consider a combination of light, medium, and dark stains to differentiate the woods. Sugar pine, douglas fir, and redwood (although a bit too soft to keep its shape after prolonged abuse and dropping) are woods that accept stains very well and should be considered by the woodworker who wishes to use economical woods for this project. All woods used in the puzzle are to be sealed, preferably with lacquer or shellac.

It should also be mentioned that sealing, varnishing, staining, etc. should be done when the project is at the point where leather is about to be attached. Accidental spillage or brush-loaded stains have a way of marking the leather, which indelibly soaks up the liquid, necessitating the cutting and installation of a new piece.

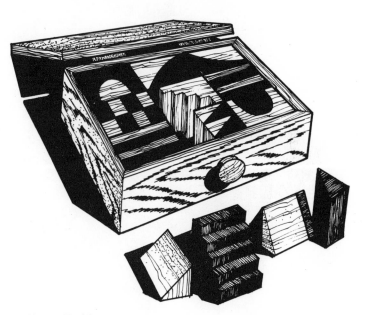

Figure III–20.
Interior view of puzzle.

Pod and Seed

Figure III–21.
Pod and Seed.

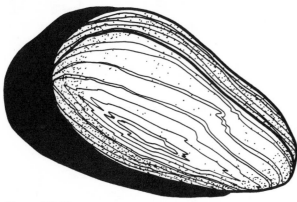

Figure III–22.
The closed pod.

A toy developed after the seed and its natural enclosure.

TOOLS

Handsaw
Wood-carving gouges *(See section on gouges.)*
Rasp
Clamp or vise
Mallet
Pencil and paper

MATERIALS

Wood
   (Use boxwood, pear wood, cherry, or pecan for the shell; use walnut, rosewood, chestnut, or cocobolo for the seed.)
   Shell: (2) 2 by 6 by 5 inches
   Seed: (1) slightly smaller than above
Clay (optional)
Sandpaper, coarse, medium, and fine grades
Steel wool, coarse, medium, and fine grades
Finishing materials *(See instructions.)*

THE TOY

To me one of the most intriguing aspects of nature is the way in which it provides seeds and other small growing life forms with a protective environment in the form of a harder enclosure to help sustain the inner growth. The egg, seashell, walnut, and chestnut are but a few examples. A project such as this one calls for a very careful examination of shape and the ways in which an object of simple form is to be cradled in its concave pocket. It also introduces the woodworker to the use of the mallet and wood-gouging tools in the most rudimentary way. It requires few materials and a steady hand. It is the kind of sculpturing experience that is within the reach of almost anyone.

The inner form (call it a "seed") may be solid or laminated. The lamination makes it more complex, but the seed can take on a dazzling appearance of light and dark wood, as involved and intriguing as you wish it to be.

The outer box (or "shell") belies the inner form. Its very rigid, almost aseptic appearance contributes all the more to the surprise that lies within.

PROCEDURE

I recommend, especially for this type of undertaking, that you work with a small amount of clay first to better plan the overall configuration of the final seed. Because the outer shell conforms to the sculpted form, it is necessary to decide on the shape of the seed first. Just as the hardened clay seed serves as the model for the wood one, so the inner form of the two half shells are dictated by the shape of the seed. After some preliminary shapes have been worked out carefully, examine them for practicality. Can the clay version be adapted to its wood counterpart? Does the carving skill exceed the experience you might have at this point in your woodworking hobby? Does the clay have an aesthetic, natural form that flows and feels good to

70

the touch? Does it fit in the contour of your palm to enable a good grip? Ask yourself any number of questions, just as you would in any problem-solving situation before deciding on the best solution.

The outer box need not be a box per se. The version illustrated shows a shell, thick walled, and substantial, which, in a less exaggerated way, follows the shape, contour, and form of the seed it is meant to hold.

Once your design has been accomplished in clay, proceed to choosing your woods and carving the pieces. If the seed is to be laminated, cut the woods to rough size, glue, clamp, and let dry. Shape the seed first, then the outside contours (if any) of the box or shell, and, finally, using the seed as a model, hollow out the inner cavity.

As in any carving project, rough hewing is done first, followed by careful sculpting with smaller, more delicate tools. Push the tool with your hand or gently assist with a mallet to dislodge the small chips. A deep gouge caused by an errant or overly aggressive mallet blow might result in your having to start all over again. Chip and tap at a comfortable pace. This is one of those woodworking projects that requires a soft but firm touch.

When the seed is finished and the exterior part of the shell is complete, the interior hollow can be carved. The seed is placed on the center of one of the wood halves. An outline of the most prominent edges (the contour) is transferred to the face of the block. The obverse side of the seed is then traced onto the other block. Both woods (halves) are clamped side by side and work with the chisels and mallet is begun. Periodically, as progress is made, place the seed into the widening and deepening pocket to further measure it for accuracy of fit. Continue making adjustments with the gouges.

Final interior work is done with coarse sandpaper for a few passes. The stiffness of the sandpaper does not lend itself to working the hills and valleys of the mold; therefore, turn to medium and fine sandpaper as you near completion of your shell. There will be a fair amount of sanding involved here as the finger traces each nodule of negative form to match the counter-positive form of the seed. Final sanding is done with coarse to fine steel wool. Once the halves are closed, the seed should rest comfortably with little movement.

FINISHING

Because of the "natural" theme, it is suggested that you do as little finishing as necessary. Some wax rubbed with the aid of cheesecloth or some preliminary rubbing and sanding with 600 Carborundum paper will give a smoother finish to all exposed surfaces. If handled frequently, oils from the palm of the hand will lubricate the wood. It will also darken slightly with time, if natural oils or waxes are used, giving the wood a refined and well-weathered appearance.

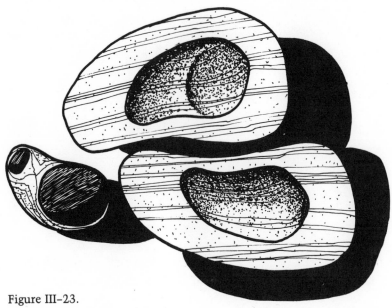

Figure III-23.
Interior view of pod and seed.

All-Terrain Train

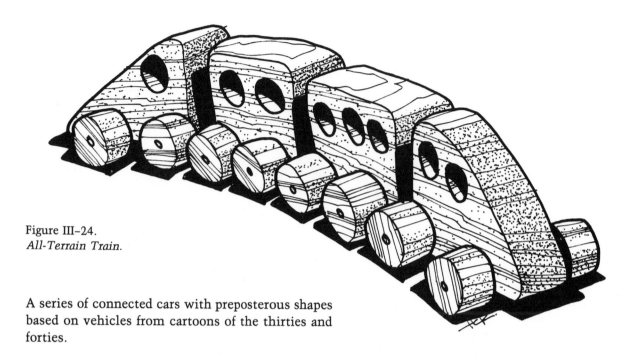

Figure III–24.
All-Terrain Train.

A series of connected cars with preposterous shapes based on vehicles from cartoons of the thirties and forties.

TOOLS
Handsaw
Coping saw
Hand drill
3/8-inch drill bit
1½-inch auger bit
Drill brace
Vise
Coarse sandpaper or rasp
Awl
Center punch
Graph paper
Ruler
French curve
Carbon paper
Pencil and paper

MATERIALS
Wood
   (Use assorted hard and softwoods of mixed color and grain. Cut wheels and axles from dowels.)
   Cars: (6) 2 by 4 by 6 inches
   Wheels: (26) 2 inches in diameter by 1 inch
   Axles: (9) 3/8 inch in diameter by 6 inches
5 small brass screw eyes
5 brass hooks to connect to screw eyes (cup hooks work well)
Finishing materials (*See instructions.*)

THE TOY
The bulbous train-car that was frequently seen in cartoons during their early gestation was somehow typified by the lack of sharp angles, gawdy hardware, and other trivial accoutrement that we associate with today's automobiles. Embodied in this all-terrain train are a car, train, snowmobile, tank, and truck all in one generalized form. It is simple, lacks any pretense, and has a very humorous look about it, as if it had been made with bread dough and had just come from the baker's oven. It is also one of those toys with which your imagination can run amok. Just about any asymmetric, lopsided shape works great.

The car-train can be as long as you wish, with as many cars as your patience allows. For the best overall look, make each car slightly different.

PROCEDURE

Design the overall shape of each car on graph paper with pencil. Transfer the measurements in your drawing to the pieces of wood, using the ruler and French curve or carbon paper. Secure each piece of wood in a vise and cut, using the coping saw. Round off all sharp edges with coarse sandpaper or a wood rasp. Mark the position of the wheels and start the axle holes with the awl. Drill all necessary holes through the cars and the wheel dowels, making each hole in the dowel exactly in the center for smooth travel.

To make the wheels permanent on the dowel axle, which should freely turn inside the car body, apply glue and let dry. It may be necessary to either sand the axle so it spins freely or use a slightly larger drill when drilling the hole through the car.

With the brace and auger bit, bore one or two holes through the shaped blocks for windows. Sand away all rough splinters both inside and out.

Add screw eyes and connecting hooks to each respective car—screw eye in front, hook in rear.

FINISHING

Apply clear polyurethane varnish to enhance the natural grain of the wood and to provide a durable surface. Stains may also be used to offset a lack of distinctive light and dark wood. Try wrapping small rubber bands around the dowel wheels for better traction.

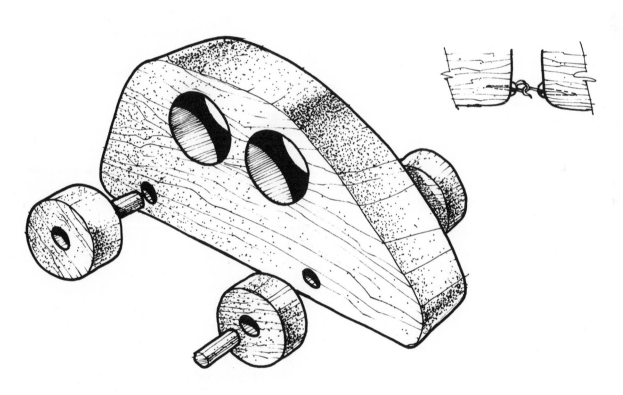

Figure III–25.
Exploded view of car and illustration of coupling device.

Laminated Milk Van

Figure III-26.
Laminated Milk Van.

A multi-layered truck made of brazilwood and oak, with yellow cedar inlay.

TOOLS
Handsaw
Coping saw
Hand drill
3/8-inch drill bit
1/8-inch drill bit
C-clamps
Wood file
Wood chisel
Wood gouge
Ruler
T square
Graph paper
Carbon paper
Pencil and paper

MATERIALS
Wood
> (Use brazilwood or other dark hardwood for 3 of the bands, oak or other light hardwood for the other 3 bands. Use yellow cedar or other light-colored softwood for inlay. Wheels, axles, and cotter pegs are to be cut from dowels.)
> Vans: (6) 1 by 9 by 9 inches
> Wheels: (4) 2 inches in diameter by ½ inch
> Axles: (2) 3/8 inch in diameter by 7 inches
> Cotter pegs: (4) 1/8 inch in diameter by 1 inch
> Inlay: (2) ¼ by 3 by 3 inches

Glue
Sandpaper, coarse, medium, and fine grades
Finishing materials (*See instructions.*)

THE TOY
This easy-to-make van requires little sawing and relies on the maker's ability to laminate alternating light- and dark-colored woods to produce a truck with a ribbon-wood effect. It is styled after the familiar boxlike, very functional milk vans, common to all neighborhoods where delivery of dairy products is still carried on.

This is a good introductory project for the woodworker who wishes to approach wood chiseling and gouging for the first time, but does so gingerly until proficiency with the tools is gained. The laminated woods make this toy a very heavy one, similar to a laminated chef's block.

Both illustrations indicate dowels or large wooden buttons for wheels. Try to locate an old rolling pin, cut it down to wheel size, and use it in place of the above two options for a more substantial set of wheels all the way around. All saw cuts are at right angles to one another. Do not overlap saw cuts, as this creates unsightly kerfs in the wood.

PROCEDURE
Plan and draw all pieces of wood to be laminated on graph paper. Transfer the measurements from the paper to each piece of wood, using carbon paper, a T square, and a pencil or carpenter's scribe. Saw all pieces of wood to size. Sandwich the woods, alternating the light and dark pieces. Apply glue to both sides of the inner pieces with thin, even strokes, covering each surface completely. Clamp the laminated block tightly with C-clamps (or Jorgenson wood clamps if available). Wipe off any glue that is oozing from the four edges of the toy.

After the block has thoroughly cured, make further cuts in the following manner: All horizontal cuts are to be 1 inch in depth; all vertical cuts are to be 2 inches in height. This covers the necessary "staircase" appearance for the front bumper, motor compartment, and cab, but these are not critical dimensions. Modify them if your cab, motor, etc., are to be either taller or shallower. File all edges with a wood file to eliminate sharp surfaces and to give the van a "softer" appearance.

Lay the van on its side and clamp it to the work table. Draw in the peripheral edges of the areas to be inlaid and begin to gouge the wood within the lines. Use a chisel to begin the cuts, making sure that the sliver or paring does not extend beyond the penciled margins. This type of accident can usually be prevented by pounding a straight-edge chisel to a depth of 1/8-inch along the pencil lines. The paring will break off at this line as the sliver comes up. Use a wood mallet to tap the wood-cutting tools. The recessed area or incised area is to be 1/8-inch deep. Sand with medium sandpaper to bring the inlay area to a flat, even surface.

Cut the piece of wood to be used for inlay, sand one side, and apply glue to the other. Position the wood in place and clamp. Notice that the cab window is left exposed; no wood is inlaid here.

Repeat the same procedure on the other side of the van. Then drill the necessary holes for the dowel axles. Before inserting the axles, sand the entire block of wood. This poses no problem since protruding parts have not been assembled. Work from the coarser sandpapers through the very fine and sand with the grain to remove saw blade and rasp marks on the wood's surface.

Insert the axles and drill holes in the wheels to fit the axle diameter. If the axle binds inside the block, sand the rod so that it will spin freely. Apply wheels and small cotter pegs. The pegs must be glued to stay in place. As with the other wheel toys, binding between the chassis and wheel can be eliminated by using a small, round piece of leather as a washer. This of course must be put in place before the cotter peg is inserted on the opposing side of the already glued end.

FINISHING

A good deal of the surface space of this toy is devoted to end grain (revealing a cross section of the original log) and inlay. If the van has been thoroughly sanded until the paper no longer serves its purpose, use coarse to fine steel wool, which can easily be maneuvered into the tighter angles and crevices.

When all abrasive work is completed, use cheesecloth to rub a good amount of paste wax vigorously into the end grain and surface grain. Much of it will be absorbed owing to the porosity of the mixed woods. Buff the surface, frequently exchanging soiled cloths for clean ones.

If you intend to lacquer the van, apply several thin, even coats, allowing each successive coat to thoroughly dry before applying additional ones. Steel-wool (grade 0000) the surface to remove bubbles and pops in the lacquer. Other sealers and finishing solutions, such as shellac, varnish, varathane, and stains, may also be used to seal or alter the surface color of the wood.

The van should be allowed to dry in a dust-free atmosphere for up to twenty four hours before it can be rolled onto the driveway and handled.

Figure III–27.
Exploded view of laminated van.

Knob and Yarn Crisscross

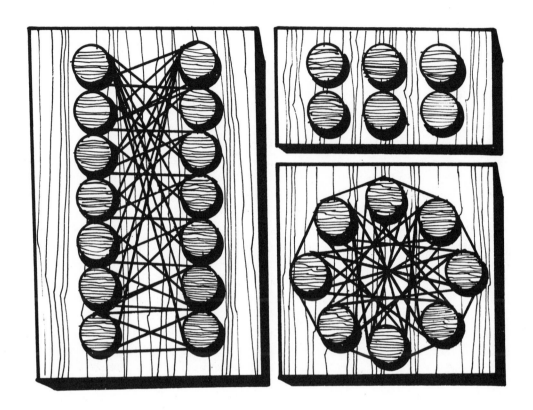

Figure III–28.
Knob and Yarn Crisscross.

Making colorful geometeric patterns with colored yarns and strings.

TOOLS
Handsaw
Hand drill
3/8-inch drill bit
Pin, tack, or brad awl
C-clamps
Ruler
T square
Pencil and paper

MATERIALS
Wood
　(Use walnut, African mahogany, or any dark hardwood.)
　Base 1 (upper left):　(1) 1 by 8 by 8 inches
　Base 2 (upper right):　(1) 1 by 4 by 8 inches
　Base 3 (bottom):　(1) 1 by 12 by 8 inches
Cabinet knobs, approximately 1 inch in diameter. dome shaped (as many as you need)
Glue
1 strip of flat wood, 1 by 1 by 12 inches
Colored yarn, string, thread, or monofilament
Finishing materials (*See instructions.*)

THE TOY

There are seemingly endless, configurations possible when a continuous piece of yarn is wrapped around knobs on a wooden base. Pictured are just a few of the ways in which the knobs can be arranged. Hexagons, triangles, octagons, pentagons, and other curious divisions of space are created. Invent your own patterns or shapes. Competitions for predetermined shapes are made possible by making two boards.

If fine string or thread is used, unravel it from the spool as you go. A pile of snarled and tangled string can bring this game to a quick halt.

This is a simple, straightforward toy requiring little woodworking skill. The base can be made more interesting by laminating different types of wood before the knobs are installed. This is a good place to get in some practical laminating experience for the first time around. Do keep the base relatively thin, however. There is no need to exceed 1-inch-thick boards. Many rare hardwoods are milled and further planed to thicknesses of ½ inch or even less. There is a point, however, where too thin a base becomes too delicate.

PROCEDURE

On a piece of paper, plot the points where the wood knobs are eventually to be glued to the board's surface. Cut the lumber to the desired size. Sand all edges, surfaces, and the bottom too. A T square or try square is useful here in making lines perpendicular to the edge of the milled stock. Place the paper on top of the base and, with a pin, tack, or brad awl, prick the paper through to the board underneath, making a small hole at each point. If you plan to countersink the stem of the knob or drawer pull, drill holes in the wood at these points. The other alternative is to simply glue the knob on top of the starter hole.

Assemble and glue all knobs in one row at a time. Position them on the board and place a long strip of thin lumber across the row touching the topmost part of each knob. Slip two C-clamps over each end of the strip. This serves as a pressure plate to keep the knobs in place while the glue is drying. If your design calls for a circular arrangement of knobs, simply position a cookie tin on top of the knobs and place several heavy books in a pile on top of the tin. Let this stand overnight. The weight will be sufficient to keep the objects firm until the glue has fully cured.

The underpart of the knob, if made of rough wood, may need to be sanded. Often, when winding yarn or string around the neck of the drawer pull, a fine splinter snares the string and makes removing it difficult. The application of a wood sealer will obviate the need for extensive sanding.

FINISHING

This game is best polished up by applying a good lacquer or varnish to all surfaces from top to bottom. It receives a lot of use, as it is designed to be worked endlessly with the hands, so take care to use a good-quality and fresh supply of varnish, shellac, lacquer, varathane, or other sealant. Use only those finishes that in no way adulterate the color of the wood if the natural color is attractive. Old varnishes, etc., tend to bring a noticeable yellow tinge to wood and can be objectionable if all you want to do is seal the pores. My recommendation for this type of finish, which you want to be as clear as possible, is to stick with the varathane liquid. It spreads well, many layers can be applied with practically no surface buildup, and artificial color due to the chemical properties of the sealer are almost negligible. Very fine steel wool will remove bubbles and fine particles that have strayed onto the finish while drying.

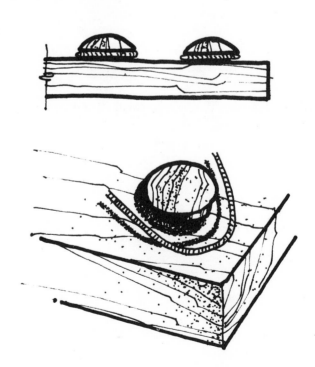

Figure III-29.
A detail of the Knob and Yarn Crisscross. This side view of the pegs on base shows the yarn about to be wrapped around the pegs.

African Thumb Piano

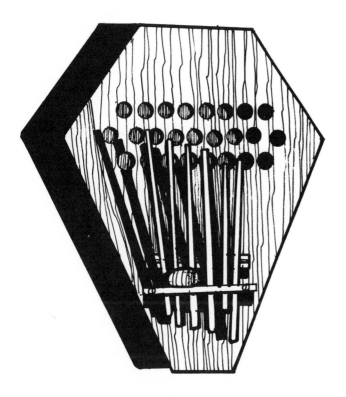

Figure III–30.
African Thumb Piano.

A traditional African musical instrument from the heart of the continent.

TOOLS
Handsaw
Backsaw
Drill
¼-inch drill bit
Brace
1-inch auger bit or 1-inch spade bit if power drill is used
Miter box
Clamps
Screwdriver
Straight-barreled awl
Ruler
Carbon paper
Pencil and paper

MATERIALS
Wood
    (Use mahogany for the instrument box, a light-colored hardwood for the tongues, and any hardwood for the bridges and brace.)
    Top and Bottom: (2) ¼ by 18 by 24 inches
    Sides: (2) ½ by 13 by 3 inches
    Sides: (2) ½ by 9 by 3 inches
    Sides: (2) ½ by 7 by 3 inches
    Tongues: (6) ¼ by ½ by 12 inches
    Bridges: (2) 1 by 1 by 4 inches
    Brace: (1) 1 by 1 by 6 inches
2 wood screws, ¼ by 1½ inches
Carpenter's hide glue
Sandpaper, medium and fine grades
Finishing materials (*See instructions.*)

THE TOY
The term "African thumb piano" is the one most frequently used to describe this unique instrument, long a fixture of the people of African nations. Native Africans call this instrument the "sansa." Each one is totally handmade in any number of designs, from decorative patterns to human effigies. The instrument can be as long as 3 to 4 feet and is capable of rich sounds. The sounds vary with the overall proportion of the instrument. The mellifluous tones of the sansa are used throughout Africa to accompany both religious and secular music. The hardwood tongues, often fashioned from bamboo, are attached to a sounding board or to a hollow box resonator, often elaborately decorated with symbolic figures. The instrument is held in the hands or arms, depending on size, and the "keys" are plucked downward with the thumbs and forefingers.

The keys are adjusted by means of loosening the top brace, which in turn is fastened to the instrument's surface below the two bridges. Each key may be moved forward or backward, which affects the length and depth of the key and note respectively.

The resonating box must be fashioned with thin woods to yield the richer notes. Much like a guitar or cello, the resonating box is an essential component of the instrument that can be experimented with again and again until you are satisfied with the sound.

Mahogany is an ideal wood for this particular instrument. However, try a few. Perhaps the hidden quality of other woods from various parts of the world will bring forth an unexpected surprise.

This instrument requires methodical planning and construction. Simpler versions are made by omitting the drilling of holes and by using string to lash the tongues in place.

Simple tunes can be quickly learned, and notes are sounded individually or simultaneously to extend the instrument's capabilities. If you enjoy making this one, consider making two more, but of different sizes—one slightly smaller, the other twice this size. The difference in sound will be noticeable.

PROCEDURE

Draw the entire outline of the top, bottom, and side pieces of the instrument on paper first to make a pattern. Check for accuracy, fit, and least amount of waste. Place the pattern on the flat pieces of wood and transfer the drawing by means of carbon paper or a scribing tool to the wood.

Saw each piece of wood to conform to your plan. Mark the wood "top," "bottom," "left side," etc., so that no piece is used in place of another.

Drill two holes in the brace, one at each end and ½ inch from each edge. Lightly sand the brace to make it as smooth as possible.

Cut and sand the tongues to size. You will note that the tongues are of identical length—each will be positioned to yield a different note.

Next, fashion the two bridges and sand. The bridges are placed on the top surface wood at about 3 to 5 inches from one another for different sounds, as desired.

Miter all edges requiring a fit of less than a 90-degree angle. The fit must be precise or the notes will be weakened, since they will escape through cracks rather than the intended holes.

Although it is better to drill three rows of 1-inch holes in the top piece before the box is assembled, this step may be performed once the box dries. The top row has eight holes, the second, nine holes, and the third, eight holes. All holes should be equidistant from one another. The advantage of drilling before assembly is that the underside of the wood can be sanded in the event the wood boring creates a burr on the edge of the hole. Although this in no way affects the sound, it does present a more tidy manner of finishing wood.

Assemble the box according to the illustration and glue and clamp in place using the hide glue. This glue is extremely strong and provides the necessary adhesion for a quality job.

Once box and holes have been made, closely examine all surface joints. If small cracks are noticed, fill them with wood paste and sand the excess.

The two bridges function as pronounced frets over which the tongues pass. Place the first bridge 3 inches from the bottom edge and parallel to it. Glue and clamp this one in place. Place the second bridge up from the first by 4 inches (anywhere between 3 to 5 inches). Glue and clamp in the same manner as the first bridge.

Arrange the tongues from left to right so that a small space separates them. There is no formula here; it is just that they are not to contact one another. For a trial run, stagger the tongues from short to long. Position the brace on top of the tongues. Fasten the brace in place by means of the two screws. Do not overly tighten, as the wood may split or further adjustments may be required.

Pluck a few of the tongues to familiarize yourself with each tone. Spacing each tongue by moving it forwards or backwards will create a higher or deeper sound.

FINISHING

Apply a wood sealer to all surfaces, including the tongues. Lightly sand to give a smooth, low sheen and to preserve the overall appearance of the wood. Wood sealer prevents moisture from seeping into the wood, which would thereby affect the sound.

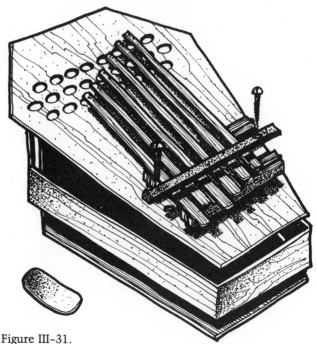

Figure III–31.
Exploded view of the toy.

Suspended Magnet and Frame

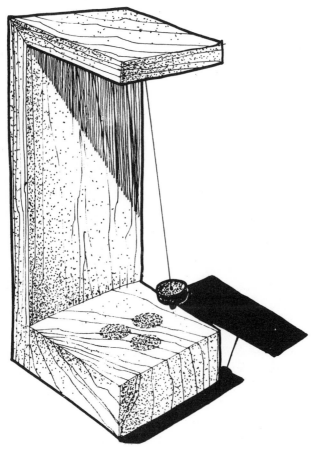

Figure III–32.
Suspended Magnet and Frame.

Four magnets are used to create the illusion that a piece of string is suspended on an angle.

TOOLS

Handsaw
Backsaw
Hand or power drill
1/8-inch drill bit
½-inch flat-spade bit
Straight-barreled awl
Miter box
Clamps
Pencil and paper

MATERIALS

Wood
   (Use hardwood or softwood.)
   Vertical piece: (1) ½ by 3 by 12 inches
   Top piece: (1) ½ by 3 by 3 inches
   Bottom piece: (1) 1 by 3 by 3 inches
1 piece of dark twine, 10¼ feet long
4 round magnets, ½ inch in diameter, ¼-inch thick
Glue
Wood filler to match color of wood
Finishing materials (*See instructions.*)

THE TOY

A piece of string with a magnet on the end is suspended from an attractive frame. Three identical magnets are countersunk just beneath the top surface of the base. As the suspended magnet swings in a pendulating manner and approaches the hidden ones, a jerking motion of string and magnet occurs.

The countersunk magnets must be placed so that the reverse side or opposing polarity effect takes place. As magnets either repel or attract one another, it is the repelling feature which causes the hanging magnet to dance and which makes this a unique toy. If the wood filler is used to effectively conceal the magnets, the onlooker is left guessing how the effect of the inclined string is created.

The salient and most attractive feature of this toy, apart from its function, is the overall simplicity of the construction and the warmth of the finished wood. The natural phenomenon of repelling magnets will take care of itself, but it remains up to the maker to embellish the wood and bring it to a state of beauty with simple and basic steps of cutting, sanding, polishing, and fitting the parts to the form.

PROCEDURE

The measurements given in the list are recommended for ease of construction and workability of the wood. The critical arrangement of space separating the hidden and exposed magnets must be worked out individually for the best results.

Cut the wood pieces to size. The top edge of the vertical piece and the top piece are to be mitered and joined at a 90-degree angle. The bottom edge is to be butt-jointed with the base.

Drill the base with three holes toward the front edge of the wood as depicted in the illustration. Leave approximately 3/8 inch of space between them. The ½-inch flat-spade bit is used to make the three holes just deep enough to insert the magnets (negative charge facing up) with a remaining space of 1/8 inch. This is to allow for the wood filler to be applied on top of the magnets, flush with the surface of the bottom piece. Choose a wood filler as close to the color of the base as possible. If necessary, rub some stain on the filled areas, if they dry lighter.

A word about the actual magnets: The magnets may take any form. However, the small, round ones I have selected are cheap and simple to work with. They are available in hardware stores, five-and-dimes, or lumberyards specializing in drawer and cabinet hardware. They are used in place of cabinet latches and are frequently used to affix papers to metal surfaces.

Drill a small 1/8-inch hole in the underside of the top piece of wood. Make the hole just above the three countersunk magnets and allow for perfect alignment between the intended string and magnet and the other magnets.

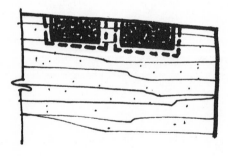

Figure III–33.
Cross section illustrating magnets inlaid into the base of the toy.

Tie a small knot in the piece of string at one end and leave the other end momentarily free. Drill a hole in the magnet to be suspended, thread the free end of the string through so that the positive charge faces down, and tie off the end with a small knot. Examine the clearance between the magnets and determine if the proximity is such that the effect of reverse polarity will cause the magnet to deflect in several directions. If this is not the case, lower the magnet by removing the string and replacing it with a longer one. If this, too, has no effect, then the concealed magnets were buried too deep and must be raised by a fraction of an inch until the polarity is strong enough to be observable. Stronger magnets will, of course, create a stronger attraction or repulsion.

Once you have determined the proper string length, clip any excess string beyond both knots. Glue the knotted, free end of the string, gently stuff it into the top hole, and leave it to dry.

FINISHING

Depending on the overall condition of the wood, sand with the appropriate sandpapers, working from medium to fine. Sand slowly and firmly with the grain to remove saw cuts and other surface scratches. Move from sandpaper to steel wool, working from coarse 0 to very fine 0000. Rottenstone and a soft cloth will further polish the wood's surface. Follow this step by applying small amounts of paste wax and rubbing the wax with a soft cloth, until a smooth and shiny luster is achieved.

Peg the Block

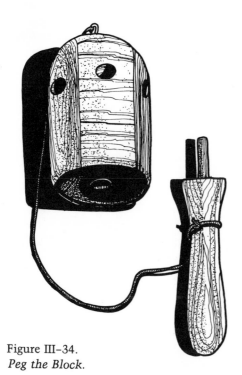

Figure III–34.
Peg the Block.

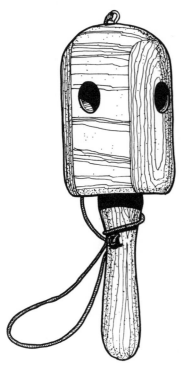

Figure III–35.
The block in place.

With one hand, attempt to peg the block with the pointed end of the stick as it swings in the air.

TOOLS

Handsaw
Hand brace or power drill
¼-inch drill bit
½-inch flat-spade bit
Surform rasp plane
Clamps
Round wood rasp
Flat wood rasp
Graph paper
Carbon paper
Pencil and paper

MATERIALS

Wood
  (Use light and dark hardwood.)
  Top: (3) 1 by 3 by 6 inches
Dowel, 2 inches in diameter by 6 inches
Carpenter's hide glue
Sandpaper, coarse, medium, and fine grades
Cord, 12 inches long (should be strong, but thin)
Small screw eye with ½-inch-long thread
Finishing materials (*See instructions.*)

THE TOY

"Peg the block" is often found in Mexico and Central America. It is a version of "ball in a cup," the objective being to catch a golf-sized ball in a small cup. Here, the skills needed are ones of perception and the ability to make sharp movements. Fitting the pointed end of the handle into any one of the holes is not as easy as it may appear to one who has not experienced this type of game. The movement of the hand is subtle, but it is the sudden jerking motion that pulls the string taut and whips the block into position so that the tip can be immediately thrust into place. The game is made all the more challenging when a particular sequence of plugging the holes must be followed by each player. The overall size of the top block must be kept reasonably small—that is, within the dimensions given. Any piece that is larger tends to become a knuckle buster should the block not be pegged right off from the start. Arrange the woods so that a "sandwich" effect is achieved with either two light or two dark woods on either side of the contrasting one. The wood may also be positioned before clamping and gluing so that the end grain faces to the side of the toy, rather than toward the top, which is the more traditional way.

PROCEDURE

Plan the overall shape of both pieces (top and handle) on paper. Use graph paper to take advantage of the coordinating lines. Transfer the measurements to the blocks of wood and dowel rod. Once the three blocks of wood have been sawed, glued, and clamped, the shaping process can begin. Although the coping saw can be used to rough out the contoured lines, a better tool to use is the Surform rasp plane. Quickly and with little effort, this tool will remove excess wood and can be used in a more sculptural fashion. The rasp lends itself to being turned with the hands and wrist and "rides" the growing round contour of the wood.

The shape of the top block should be slightly oblong, similar to a lawn mallet, but more rounded. No sharp edges should remain. Drill ½-inch holes on four sides and the bottom of the block. Clamp the block to a drilling surface for this step. It is simpler to drill the holes through the wood from one side to the other, rather than having to gauge each bore for the respective sides.

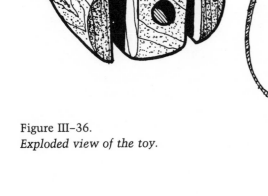

Figure III–36.
Exploded view of the toy.

Continue to file and sand the block until a round shape is achieved. When the wood has been made smooth, predrill a small hole in the top center of the block to receive the screw eye. Install the screw eye so that nothing of the shank is left showing.

The handle is modeled by means of the round and flat wood rasp to give the wood its shape. The handle should fit comfortably in the hand and should be smooth to the touch. The tapered tip must be worked so that the diameter is smaller than the actual hole it is meant to fit. This allows for free play. It would be extremely difficult to fit both peg and hole if no margin or tolerance of play was permitted. The tapered portion of the handle measures 1 inch in length and has a diameter of 3/8 inch or slightly less.

Attach cord to the top end of the block by means of the screw eye and tie with a square knot. Drill the handle with a hole passing from one side to the other. Sand the hole and insert the other end of the string. Tie a large enough knot on this end to prevent the string from escaping. Periodically wax the string to keep it from unraveling.

FINISHING

Finish the wood in the usual manner. After sanding with fine sandpaper, work the surface with 00 steel wool. Proceed to 0000 steel wool and carnauba paste wax. Work the wax into the surface and let stand for an hour. Wipe the excess wax off with a soft cloth, apply a small amount of the wax heated to the touch, and massage the wood with another cloth with a soft nap until a good luster is achieved.

If a clear finish is desired, refer to **Finishes** to choose the best means of sealing and finishing the toy.

Tic-Tac-Toe
(Upright Version)

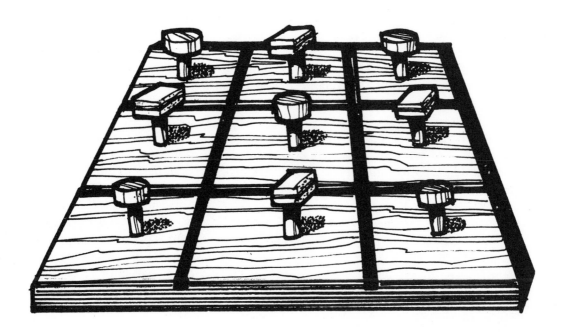

Figure III–37.
Tic-Tac-Toe (Upright Version).

A traditional lap game with pegs, circles, and squares added for a new twist.

TOOLS
Handsaw
Hand drill (brace)
3/8-inch drill bit
C-clamps
Keyhole file
Sandpaper, grades 120 and 220
Ruler or try square
Pencil and paper

MATERIALS
Wood
   (Use 2 pieces each of light and dark wood for base. Also, half the squares should be dark and half should be light. Circles are cut from a dowel.)
   Base: (4) ½ by 10 by 10 inches
   Circles: (10) 1 inch in diameter by 5 inches
   Squares: (10) ¼ by 1 by 1 inch
Dowel, 3/8 inch in diameter by 10 inches
White glue or carpenter's hide glue
Finishing materials (*See instructions.*)

THE TOY
This version of tic-tac-toe is a direct offshoot of noughts and squares, where two opponents play in turn and try to position three of their symbols in a straight line—horizontally, vertically, or diagonally.

The boxes are divided by a kerf line and all squares and circles are raised off the playing board by means of short pieces of dowel.

This is a very simple game to make, requiring only a few tools. The subtle beauty of the board is achieved by laminating light and dark wood. The kerf saw line or dado cut exposes the light wood laminated beneath the dark wood. All surfaces are oiled and highly polished to make them appealing to the eye, as well as a delight upon which to play.

PROCEDURE
Cut lumber to size. Apply glue to the surfaces of the wood to be laminated. It makes no difference which wood is on top—light or dark. Clamp the two pieces of wood together and let dry. Remove clamps and divide the board into nine equal sectors with a ruler or try square. Locate the center of each square by means of two lines drawn from each corner of the

84

square to form an "x." With the 3/8-inch drill bit, drill a hole at the intersection of each x to a depth of ¼ inch.

Clamp the playing board to the worktable. With a handsaw or backsaw, cut thin dado lines along the pencil lines just deep enough to expose the contrasting wood. If the dado line is thin, make an auxiliary cut just to the right or left of the original line to widen it. (Of course, if your shop is equipped with a radial-arm saw or a table saw, a dado attachment will perform the task with ease.) Sand all edges with burrs by means of a keyhole file or by inserting sandpaper into the groove and gradually working the paper back and forth with short strokes. The grooves should be approximately 1/8 inch in width.

Cut, glue, and laminate the small wood squares to form the tops of the pegs. (For each of the five squares laminate a dark and a light piece.) Clamp until dry. Cut ½-inch sections of dowel rod from the 5-inch-long strip, making a total of five circles. Sand all pieces of wood.

Glue both square and round tops to the 3/8-inch dowel pegs. There will be a total of ten pegs of 1-inch length.

Try the pegs in the bored holes and check for a snug, but removable, fit. Additional sanding may be required to bring about a smoother movement between pegs and drilled holes.

FINISHING

An oil-varnish may be applied to the board. However, the oil, if pigmented, will darken both laminated pieces considerably. Use a clear finish, such as polyurethane or shellac, for a durable surface. Avoid shellace if the game is likely to come into contact with moisture, as it may make the shellac loose and tacky. Aerosol lacquer or lacquer can be applied by means of a small compressor, which will assist you in that it helps get the sealer in difficult-to-reach places such as the dado grooves.

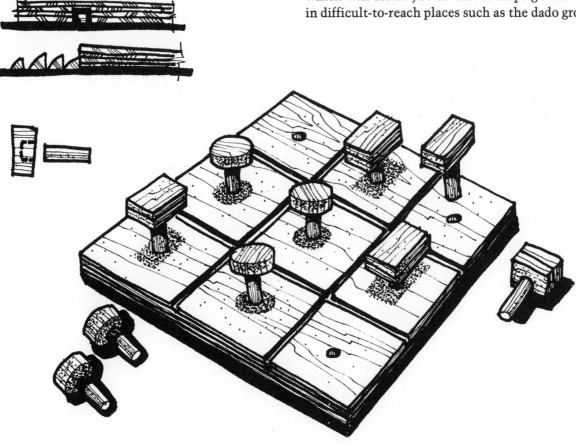

Figure III–38.
Another view of board and pieces plus detail of dadoing procedure for scoring the game board.

Push-and-Pull Locomotive and Bin Cars

Figure III–39.
Push-and-Pull Locomotive and Bin Cars.

A workable wooden toy for all ages. Make a dozen bins to carry all sorts of small odds and ends.

TOOLS

Handsaw
Backsaw
Hand or power drill
½-inch drill bit
3/8-inch drill bit
Miter box
Mallet
Clamps
Wood rasp
Ruler
Pencil and paper

MATERIALS

Wood
   (Use a light hardwood for the engine and any hardwood for the rest. The axles, wheels, and steam chute are cut from wheels.)
   Engine: (1) 3 by 5 by 6 inches
   Each bin car: (5) ½ by 4 by 4 inches
   Caboose: (1) 4 by 4 by 4 inches
   Caboose cabin: (1) ½ by 3 by 3 inches
   Cattle guard: (1) 3 by 1 by 1½ inches
   Each axle: (1) 3/8 inch in diameter by 4 inches
   Each wheel: (1) 1 inch in diameter by ½ inch
   Steam chute: (1) ½ inch in diameter by 3 inches
Screw eyes to connect cars
String to connect screw eyes
Glue
Finishing materials (*See instructions.*)

THE TOY

A train such as this is one of the staple items in any woodworker's collection of toys made. The train can be fitted with any number of different cars and can be converted into a logger, tanker, stake body car, coal car, or whatever the imagination comes up with. A train of this design is reminiscent of the narrow-gauge machines that used to puff their way through the remote European countryside. In many out-of-the-way places these trains still exist.

The sideward twisting of the cars is achieved by means of lashing together the screw eyes on the front and back of each car by means of a bit of twine. The largest car is the locomotive, which is made from a square piece of wood. You simply round off the front portion of the locomotive by means of a wood rasp to provide the necessary body styling.

PROCEDURE

Mark all wood pieces with lines for cutting and cut with the handsaw. The pieces must be straight to effect a good joint. Use the miter box and handsaw when cutting the mitered edges for the bin cars. At this scale, the mitered look is more convincing than the butt-end joint. Glue the four sides of the bins together, position, and clamp. Repeat the process for every bin car. The bottoms will be positioned later.

Divide the block for the locomotive in half by means of a pencil line. Round the forward half with the wood rasp to resemble the front end of the train pictured in the illustration. Leave the back half as is.

Cut the cattle guard with a wedge shape toward the front to give it a "scooped" look. The cattle guard is as wide as the locomotive.

Make the caboose car by centering the smaller piece on the 4- by 4- by 4-inch block. Glue, clamp, and let dry. Measure and drill the holes through which the axles will be placed. Drill ½-inch-diameter holes in the bins, the locomotive, and the caboose. The locomotive has three holes, instead of the usual two. Cut all axles from the dowel rod, each measuring 4 inches long. Cut all wheels from the 1-inch-diameter dowel, each one measuring ½ inch.

Drill all dowels that are to be used as wheels using the 3/8-inch bit. The bore must be in the center of the dowel to keep the wheel's motion "in round." Add the bottom panels to the bins, glue, and clamp in place.

Drill a hole in the top on the rounded portion of the locomotive toward the front edge for the steam chute. Glue the dowel and place it in the hole. The front of the locomotive also has a small piece of dowel applied to the face of the wood to suggest a headlight.

Insert axles through train cars. Put a small amount of glue on each dowel end and tap wheels in place with the mallet. The axles must spin freely to enable the train to move along to its next destination. Sand all surfaces and bring each car to the usual finishing state.

FINISHING

Apply wax and buff to a sheen to give the train a hand-polished look. Spray lacquer or an oil stain is appropriate for those situations where the wood lacks any distinctive visual qualities or when the wood is toned to make it resemble a more exotic wood. Oil stains must be worked into the surface of the wood and rubbed every few days to give a convincing finish to the overall toy. Stain must be worked quickly. If not, streaks occur, and, unless they are to be construed as grain lines, they are undesirable.

Figure III–40.

Exploded view of bin cars and detail of coupling mechanism.

Weights and Balances

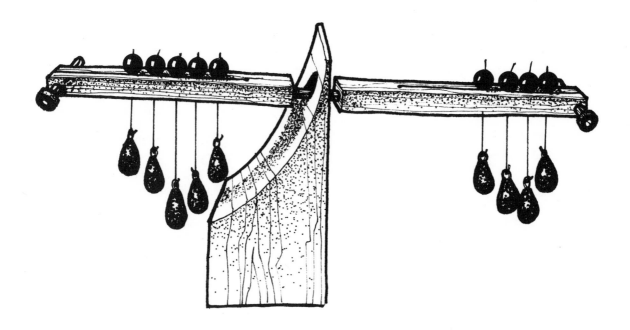

Figure III–41.
Weights and Balances.

A game requiring delicate touch and visual accuracy.

TOOLS
Handsaw
Coping saw
Keyhole saw
Hand drill or power drill
¼-inch drill bit
5/8-inch drill bit or auger bit
Sandpaper, grades 120 and 220
Ruler
Carbon paper
Pencil and paper

MATERIALS
Wood
   (Use any dark hardwood. Cut fulcrum and cotter keys from dowels.)
   Base: (1) 4 by 4 by 6 inches
   Parallel levers: (2) 2 by 2 by 10 inches
   Fulcrum: (1) 3/8 inch in diameter by 6 inches
   Cotter Keys: (2) ¼ inch in diameter by 5 inches
2 small rubber washers (to slip over cotter keys)
10 fisherman's sinkers, 1 to 2 ounces each
10 rubber balls, approximately ¾ inch in diameter
Strong twine or fine monofilament, 4 feet long
Glue
Finishing materials (*See instructions.*)

THE TOY

Balancing games test the skill of the players, but a game of this design may be played individually. The materials used for its construction are commonly available from hardware and sporting-goods stores. If you look closely, you will see that the fulcrum is made of a small dowel rod connecting two larger pieces, which both have channels cut through them. The player moves the weights back and forth along the groove to evenly distribute the weight.

The principle is quite simple; adjusting the weights so that the bar remains level with the surface isn't.

The base in the illustration is asymmetrical. However, you may want to design one that is triangular or rectangular in shape. Whatever you decide, the top portion is to be narrow to allow for the up-and-downward motion of the parallel lever. Use a good, heavy hardwood for the base. The cross members may be of any wood. Light-colored woods look best for contrast. Avoid any extremely hard wood such as oak or walnut for these pieces as the cutting of the channel will be further complicated by hard fibers and grain. Of course, if you are equipped with the right tools, this bit of caution does not apply.

The construction time for this project is 2½ hours, but be prepared to make lots of these for interested friends.

PROCEDURE

In order to ensure accuracy in measuring and dimensioning the wood for the base, the best technique is to make all preliminary drawings on paper, then transfer the guide lines to the stock. Regardless of how you want to shape the wood base, the base must be larger than the top. The point is that the added weight of the lead sinkers must never overcome the base or it will topple over.

Once the base has been shaped, bore a 5/8-inch hole near the top through which the fulcrum dowel arm will pass. Sand all rough edges.

The two parallel levers are to be divided down the center to within 1 inch of one end. Using the handsaw, make a kerf cut in the stock, entering from the opposite end. This is the grooved path along which the weights will travel. Plan to make the groove about ¼ inch wide.

Connect both levers by means of the fulcrum dowel strip. Drill the grooved end of both levers to a depth of 1 inch using the ¼-inch drill bit. Insert the fulcrum dowel into the end. Then insert the doweled lever through the predrilled hole at the top of the base. Place the other end of the dowel into the other lever, thereby connecting the two levers.

Tie a knot close to one end of each string and slip a rubber ball through each string to the knot. Thread the strings through the groove and attach the weights.

Cut the cotter key dowel in half so that each one is 2½ inches long. Each end of the kerf is closed by means of insertion of the small dowel strip. A stopper is then applied to the dowel strip.

The game is now ready to be played.

FINISHING

After the wood has been brought to the usual state of a smooth surface, it may be finished by means of rubbing with paste wax or lacquered for a more protective surface.

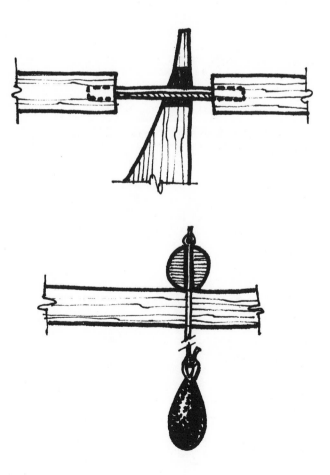

Figure III–42.
Detail of balancing rod and weight assembly.

Laminated Spinning Top

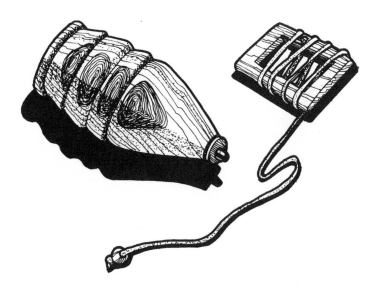

Figure III–43.
Laminated Spinning Top.

The traditional toy brought up-to-date for the experienced woodworker who is equipped with a lathe.

TOOLS
Wood-turning chisels (diamond, skew, round-nose)
C-clamps
Glue
Flat metal file
Wire nippers

MATERIALS
Wood
    (Use 2 blocks of dark hardwood and 1 block of light hardwood.)
    (2) 1 by 6 by 4 inches
    (1) 2 by 6 by 4 inches
1 sixpenny box nail
Glue
Sandpaper, grades 120 and 220
Paste wax
Finishing materials *(See instructions.)*

THE TOY
It is not certain just where the top first appeared. There is some evidence to indicate that the top was present in ancient Egypt, Greece, and Rome, and old prints show that the top has been used in Europe since the sixteenth century. It is clear that in Japan the top is the most popular toy of its kind. Top play has become a true art form there and is taken quite seriously as an exercise in concentration. Professional top spinning was very common in the Orient even before westernization took hold. Most of the Oriental tops today are started with a string and the one pictured here is based on this principle.

There are many varieties of tops. In the string-propelled type, the string is wound near the point and the top is built so that its major weight is above the spindle. The hand-twirled top, on the other hand, is designed to include the long spindle at the head of the top, rather than at the base or foot. It appears that these hand-twirled tops were first used by children. (Early illustrated accounts picture young Japanese playing with whirling tops made from bamboo and acorns.) Twirling tops are the only ones at all common with American children.

Unfortunately, not many tops are available today. There is a top that makes a humming noise as it travels down a twisted spindle held by the hand, but no effort is required to get the top to balance, and so, today's players lose an opportunity to acquire an interesting skill.

Designing a top requires some basic understanding of spinning objects and how weight is distributed for a sustained twirling movement. The foot of the top must have a tapered tip designed so that it will be as friction free as possible and will not be likely to wear for a long period. The heavier mass is usually centered from the middle and up. A well-designed top is symmetrical in weight, but not necessarily in shape. A smooth surface also contributes to a swirling performance, and it behooves the craftsman to bring the surface to a fine luster.

PROCEDURE
Laminate the three blocks of wood with hide glue and clamp tightly. Apply two pieces of wood to the foot and head. These serve as a faceplate and backing block. The 2-inch faceplate and backing block are attached to a piece of wood of smaller diameter, with a piece of paper glued between the two. This permits a clean separation of the two pieces of wood and eliminates the hole marks that remain when the faceplate is glued to the block. Stabilize the

block on the lathe and begin to shape with the wood-turning chisels.

As every woodworker who has turned stock on a lathe knows, the block, because of its rectangular shape, creates considerable vibration until the preliminary form takes shape. When shaping is completed, the sanding process can begin. Begin sanding with 120 grade paper while the stock is still in position on the lathe and continue with a finer paper, such as 220 grade, until smooth. The top is guaranteed an even finish following this technique and this is a great deal easier than turning the top manually and having to sand at the same time.

When sanding with the finest sandpaper has been completed, remove the top, faceplate, and backing block.

FINISHING

Although some woodworkers prefer to apply finishing oils with a soft cloth while the wood is still turning on the lathe, it is advisable to see to what extent the finishing oils have been absorbed by the wood. Examine the foot of the top to be sure the paper has been parted. It is not necessary to fill the small hole as the nail is installed here.

The sixpenny box nail is driven straight into the bottom of the top to a depth of 1 inch. If the nail is crooked, the top will not spin smoothly but will follow an erratic pattern. The setting of the nail is crucial to the success of the top. Clip the head of the nail with the metal nippers. The exposed portion of the nail is ½ inch in length. Place the top in a clamp, carefully wrapping it to prevent damage to the finish. Using a flat metal file, sharpen the nipped end of the nail to make a blunt point. Finish polishing the point with emery paper.

If, after a few trys, the top will not spin smoothly, make small adjustments in the nail by angling a few degrees to correct for its uneven motion. Check to be sure that you have wrapped the string tautly around the nipped waist portions of the top.

The top can be spun manually by grasping the top portion and giving the top a quick flick of the wrist, which will set it spinning. There is also the string method, whereby the string is wrapped around the top and grasped fully by the hand. Loop the topmost part of the string around the finger and pitch the top to the ground on an angle, letting the string quickly unravel as you do so. This motion accelerates the spinning and gives it the necessary momentum to keep it going.

In place of string, consider a thin strip of leather with a square piece of wood on the other end as shown. This combination will give the top a longer performance with little likelihood of the leather snapping in the midst of a pitching-spinning motion.

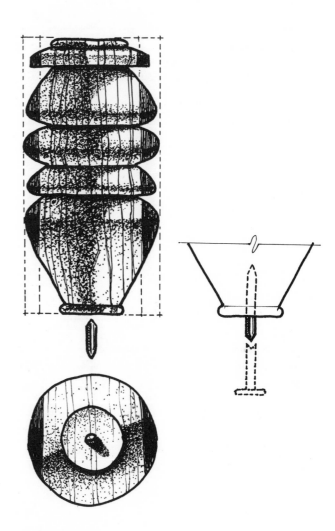

Figure III-44.
Exploded view of top and view from below. Detail shows how point is made from a nail.

Whirling Helicopter

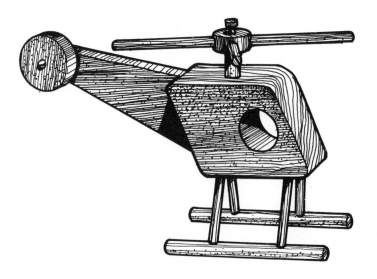

Figure III–45.
Whirling Helicopter.

Here is a toy in the form of a helicopter, a relatively new addition to the airplane toy group, unaffected by frills. This version has a rotary blade that actually spins.

TOOLS
Handsaw
Coping saw
Hand or power drill
¼-inch drill bit
½-inch drill bit
2-inch flat-spade bit
Clamps
Graph paper
Ruler
Pencil and paper

MATERIALS
Wood
(Use light-colored softwood, such as yellow pine, spruce, sugar pine, yew, etc. Rotary blades, rotary blade discs, rotary blade connector, ground rails, ground rail struts, rear rotary disc rod, and rear rotary disc are cut from dowels.)
Cabin: (1) 2 by 4 by 4 inches
Rotary blades: (3) 3/8 inch in diameter by 5½ inches
Rotary blade disc: (1) 1 inch in diameter by ½ inch
Rotary blade connector: (1) ½ inch in diameter by 1¾ inches
Ground rails: (2) 3/8 inch in diameter by 5 inches
Ground rail struts: (4) ¼ inch in diameter by 3 inches
Tail section: (1) 1 by 4 by 6 inches
Rear rotary disc rod: (1) ¼ inch in diameter by ¾ inch
Rear rotary disc: (1) 1 inch in diameter by ½ inch
Glue
Sandpaper, grades 120 and 220
Finishing materials *(See instructions.)*

THE TOY
The design of the helicopter enables it to lift vertically and move horizontally in any direction. Helicopters are also capable of hovering due to their large motor-driven rotary blades mounted horizontally. This particular helicopter design is bound to become a favorite to all who like aircraft.

PROCEDURE
Plan the cab on graph paper. Transfer the markings to the side face of the stock and mark the edge of the stock for sawing. Cut the cab free from the block, place on one side, and clamp. With the 2-inch flat-spade bit, bore a hole through the center of the diamond-shaped cab. Lightly sand around the perimeter of the hole to remove fibrous parts of wood. At a 45-degree angle, drill four ½-inch holes, two on each side on the bottom edge of the cab. The holes should be spaced 1½ inches apart from each other, and the depth of each hole need not exceed ½ inch. On the top of the cab, in the center, drill a ½-inch hole, 1 inch deep, and insert a 1¾-inch length dowel. If the fit is loose, add glue. Drill the rotary blade connector disc on its side edge in three equidistant places. Spread a small amount of glue in these holes and fit with the three rotary blades,

which have been cut from a dowel. Drill the disc in the center with a ½-inch hole fully penetrating the wood. This in turn is fitted over the dowel protruding from the top side of the cab. A few preliminary turns of the rotary blade apparatus will tell you if the protruding dowel needs some sanding.

Install rail struts and ground rails with a small dab of glue.

Cut the tail section to fit the illustration, tapering toward the top side and rounding on the end by means of sandpaper. Drill a ¼-inch hole near the rear tip and fit with the rear rotary disc rod. Apply glue first to ensure permanency. Slip the rear rotary blade disc over the dowel and glue in place.

Attach the tail assembly to the cab assembly by applying enough glue to the surfaces where they are to connect. Because of the irregular shape of the tail assembly, it may be necessary to stretch a rubber band around the entire toy to keep both glued parts under pressure while drying. Allow the toy to stand until the glue has fully cured. If a good hide glue is used under the recommended conditions, the bond will in all likelihood be as strong as the wood itself.

FINISHING

Spray or brush with lacquer for a clear and glossy finish. Wax may be used in place of the lacquer and brought to a semigloss finish with vigorous buffing with a soft cloth. The wax does not impart a hard surface to the wood as does the lacquer.

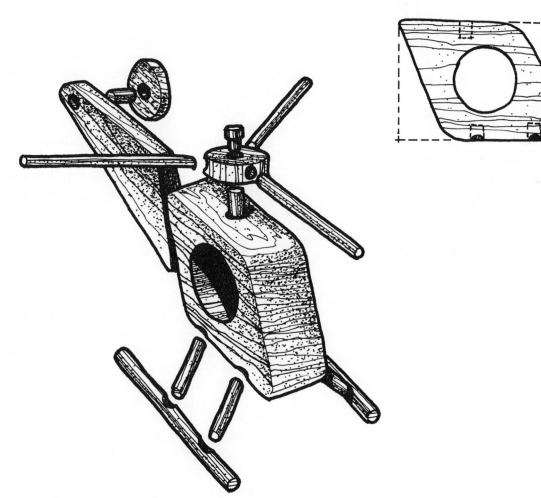

Figure III–46.
Exploded view of the helicopter.

Zebrawood Hobbyhorse

Figure III–47.
Zebrawood Hobbyhorse.

A mighty contender, along with the yo-yo, sling-shot, and spinning top, for the all-time favorite toy.

TOOLS
Handsaw
Coping saw
Hand or power drill
½-inch drill bit
1-inch flat-spade bit
Scissors
Bar clamps or pipe clamps
Soft-faced mallet
Carbon paper
Paper and pencil

MATERIALS
Wood
  (Use zebrawood for the block, light-colored hard-wood for wheels, and dark wood for eyes. Cut the axle from a dowel.)
  Stick: hardwood broom handle, 1 inch in diameter by 5 feet
  Face: (1) 2 by 4 by 8 inches
  Mane: long bristle broom, 6 inches long
  Eyes: (2) ½ by ½ by ¾ inch
  Axle: ½ inch in diameter by 6 inches
  Wheels: (2) 1 by 4 by 4 inches
Leather strip for bridle, 24 inches long
2 leather or suede scraps for ears, 3 by 5 inches
Sandpaper, grades 120 and 220
Carpenter's hide glue
Finishing materials *(See instructions.)*

THE TOY
The hobbyhorse transposes a child from the pedestrian world to one in which he rides upon a gallant mare. The hobbyhorse incites the child to gallop, trot, and run, all at his own pace and speed. It doesn't seem to matter that the toy is pulled rather than ridden upon. The child's imagination surmounts the seemingly impossible, the horse is real, alive. It has a name, true personality, and, as the day draws to a close, the hobbyhorse is corralled in the corner of the bedroom until it is mounted again.

Traditionally, the hobbyhorse has been made of stuffed software—cloth, linen, knitted yarn, leather, and burlap. The intriguing use of buttons, shells, bone, glass, or old coins, provided that proverbial facial expression of strength and gentility; no matter how crude or sophisticated the design, that expression always surfaced. Once, it was the favored toy that parents built for their children. Now, the store bought version, with its printed plastic face stapled to a hollow plastic pole, has supplanted the original ones made of wood and hardy knock-about stuff.

Here is a simple hobbyhorse you can build in a few hours to launch an assault on its plastic, molded imitators.

PROCEDURE

Transfer all markings and plans from paper to the side and edges of the rectangular block of wood. Cut free the head from the surrounding wood by means of the handsaw and coping saw. Sand any rough spots. On the neck area of the horse head, using a flat-spade bit, drill a 1-inch-wide hole to a depth of 2 inches, about 2 inches in from the back of the head. At a later time, the pole will be inserted here. Drill a second hole ½ inch in diameter near the front muzzle of the horse head. The bridle will be threaded through this hole and both ends will be tied together.

Saw a 4-inch-long section of the broom head and glue and clamp it to the back of the horse's head using bar or pipe clamps. Repeat the same procedure for the top of the mane, using a 2-inch section of the broom in this instance. Cut two leaf-shaped pieces of leather or suede for the ears and glue them to the back of the head, just below the top surface. The ears can also be mounted with two small box nails to keep them in place.

Drill a 5/8-inch hole at the bottom of the broom handle. Place the dowel in the hole and push it

the broom handle. Cut the two wheels from the 4- by 4-inch pieces of stock, using a saw. Sand wheels until smooth. Drill ½-inch-diameter holes in the two wheel discs and slip them on both ends of the axle. Glue the wheels in place; the rolling motion will occur by means of the axle turning, rather than the wheels.

Insert the broom handle through the hole of the horse's head after having applied a liberal amount of hide glue beforehand. Wipe away any residual glue as it oozes from the joint.

Drill two holes, one on each side of head, to a such as black walnut or ebony by tapping the pieces in with a mallet. The eyes may remain flush with the surface or may protrude with the ends sanded to give a more natural look.

Saddle 'em up and ride.

FINISHING

This is one of the few toys where little, if any, finishing is necessary. The application of clear lacquer, or a few coats of wax rubbed smooth with a buffing cloth, will redeem the natural appeal of the wood and preserve the toy's honest look.

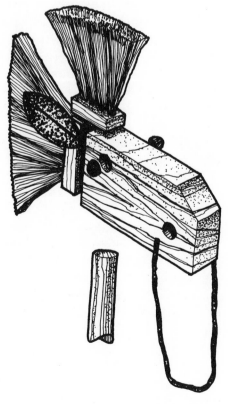
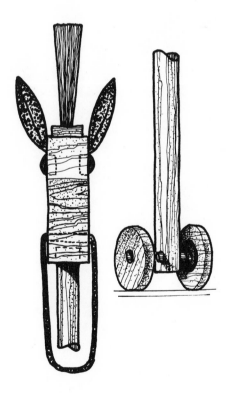

Figure III–48.
Exploded view of hobbyhorse and drawings showing detail of wheel assembly and front view of horse's head.

Marble and Maze Game

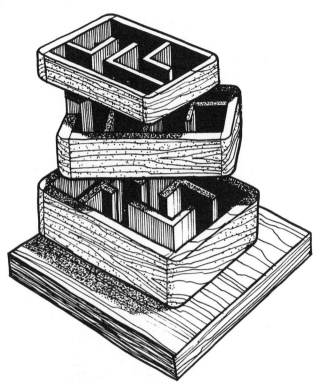

Figure III–49.
Marble and Maze Game.

By manipulating three playing boards, the player moves a marble from the top board to the bottom board but must do so by using the correct pathway in a series of mazes.

TOOLS

Handsaw
Hand drill or brace
½-inch auger or flat-spade bit
1-inch auger or flat-spade bit
Soft-faced mallet
Clamps
Needle-nosed pliers
Ruler
Graph paper
Carbon paper
Paint and paintbrush
Pencil and paper

MATERIALS

Wood
  (Use a clear, light softwood.)
  Top maze: (2) 2 by 4 by 6 inches
            (2) 2 by 4 by 4 inches
  Middle maze: (2) 2 by 4 by 8 inches
               (2) 2 by 4 by 6 inches
  Bottom maze: (2) 2 by 4 by 10 inches
               (2) 2 by 4 by 8 inches
  Base: (2) 1 by 12 by 12 inches
  Connector stems: (4) 2 by 2 by 2 inches
  Walls of maze: About 18 feet of ¼- by 1½-inch stock cut in lengths to suit your design requirements
Masonite
  Panel for top maze: (1) ¼ by 4 by 6 inches
  Panel for middle maze: (1) ¼ by 6 by 8 inches
  Panel for bottom maze: (1) ¼ by 8 by 10 inches
3 universal connectors (available from hardware stores) of the ball and socket type, about 1 inch in diameter
Glue
Marble or ball bearings
Finishing materials *(See instructions.)*

THE GAME

The objective of the game is to move each maze vertically and horizontally in such a manner as to move the marble through the maze and out the hole in the floor panel, only to fall into another even more complex maze. Here the motions are continued until it reaches the hole in the second maze. The third and largest maze contains a hole in one corner for the last drop. The difficulty is further compounded when the player works against the clock.

PROCEDURE

It is crucial to the success of your three-platform toy that the mazes be worked out on paper before construction begins. Consult one of numerous books available on maze puzzles, often found in children's literature and game books. Graph paper can be used to scale placement of the walls to minimize confusion and error. Draw a plan for each maze and transfer dimensions to the respective masonite panel. In order to make lines visible for the maze assembly brush on a light coat of paint on the upper surface of each panel. This way, your pencil lines will be more evident.

Glue and clamp together the sides of each of the three mazes. Do the small maze first, and so on. Once the rectangular frame is made, apply a small bead of glue along the bottom edge of each frame and press on each Masonite floor panel. Use long clamps of the adjustable type, if available, and clamp the Masonite floor to frame.

With needle-nosed pliers, grasp any one of a variety of walls that have been cut to the planned length. Apply glue to the bottom edge and put in premarked space. Each maze is slowly and carefully built to ensure the marble's free travel and that all walls are upright and firmly bonded.

Drill an exit hole large enough for the marbles or ball bearings to fall freely through each floor panel at the points you have designated.

Next, glue and clamp one of the connector stems to the underside of the top and middle mazes. (See finishing instructions before connecting.) Follow this by gluing and clamping a connector stem to the top face of the middle and bottom mazes.

Drill a hole the same size as the universal joint stems (about 1 inch) in those connectors that interface, and install the universal joint connector to permit free movement of each maze panel. (The detail to the right of the large drawing illustrates this step.) Tap the universal joint with a lightweight mallet to drive the pinions in the predrilled holes. No glue is necessary.

Some universal joints require occasional lubrication with a drop of 3-in-1 oil to keep the movement loose and minimize friction.

FINISHING

If finishing by sanding, it is best to perform this step before the parts are put together. You might want to spray-paint the entire toy to sidestep some difficult and delicate sanding and brush application of oils or sealers. Select a lacquer that is lightly pigmented if you want, or spray glaze will do the job nicely. Access to a small compressor of ¾ horsepower will provide enough pressure when coupled with an airbrush.

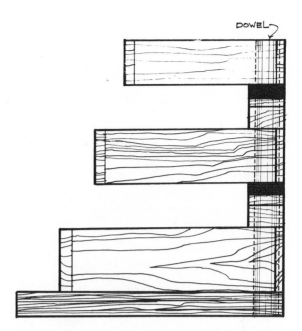

Figure III–50.
Detailed view of dowel assembly.

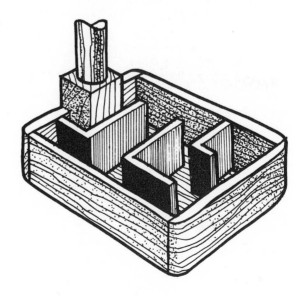

Figure III–51.
Top view of maze, illustrating position of walls and hole for marble, and detail of middle maze.

Jack-in-the-Box

Figure III–52.
Jack-in-the-Box.

Figure III–53.
The closed box.

Another time-honored movement toy. A jack-in-the-box is simply a spring figure arranged inside a box so that it will jump out when the cover is raised.

TOOLS
Handsaw
Backsaw
Miter box
Clamps
Flat wood chisel
Screwdriver
Sewing tools

MATERIALS
Wood
   (Use mixed dark and light, hard and softwoods. Small pieces of wood from the scrap bin can be assembled into 6 pieces, each measuring 10 by 10 by ½ inch.)
2 flat brass universal hinges, 1 inch wide
Cloth and trimmings to make a small clown (to fit inside box)
Coiled spring (to be of tapered shape to fit inside the clown. The tension of the spring is to be adjustable.)
Carpenter's hide glue
2 wood screws
Finishing materials *(See instructions.)*

THE TOY
The jack-in-the-box is known by various names, such as ''Punch Box,'' ''Surprise Box,'' ''Admiral on a Stick,'' or ''Johnny Jump Up.'' Most of the early jack-in-the-boxes were designed with hideous figures. The idea was to frighten the unsuspecting child as the figure suddenly popped up. Once children learned the trick they took particular delight in snapping the lid open in the face of adults—usually the same adults who gave them the toy in the first place.

It is thought that the toy was developed by the German toy industry. It became a household favorite during the eighteenth and nineteenth centuries in Europe, to reach this country only by the late 1800s. Unlike the versions sold at the toy counter today, in which a grinding lever with accompanying melody is employed, jack-in-the-boxes were of a simpler nature, fright and all. The version constructed here is more like the early jack-in-the-box and is opened at will. A more friendly face pops up and replaces the horrific ones of years ago.

PROCEDURE
The toy is built in two phases. The first phase involves the building of the box; the second, the making of the clown. The coiled spring will be installed in the bottom of the box, and the puppet will be slipped over the spring while the box lid forces the puppet down.

Lay out the pieces of wood for each side of the box according to grain, wood color, and the swirling direction of the growth patterns of the wood. Arrange them to please yourself and to show that woods of very different and unique origins can be used to complement one another, rather than to compete with one another.

Saw all pieces of wood to size. The woods are of uniform thickness. Apply glue to each side edge, clamp, and place each side of the box in an area to fully dry. The edges of the four sides are then mitered and joined with hide glue. Clamp the entire box, rather than two sides at one time. The bottom of the box is one solid piece of wood. Before inserting in the bottom of the box, attach the coil spring by means of a small piece of flexible metal strip (such as perforated plumbers' strap) over the bottom coil. Fasten each end of the strap to the wood with two small wood screws. Install the bottom panel, having applied a thin bead of glue to the surfaces where the joint is to be made.

The top panel is laminated with mixed woods in the same manner as the four sides. With the wood chisel, lightly remove thin parings of wood to make two notches to receive the hinges. This is done on the underside of the lid, at the back edge, as well as on the top rear edge of the box. They must align. Install the hinges by means of the screws usually supplied with the hinges.

Make the clown of ruffled material designed to conceal the spring. Colorful fabric makes the clown gayer and can be as imaginative in its construction as you want. Facial expressions are important to the overall effect of the "surprise," since it is usually the face the child responds to first of all. Buttons, small wood, or glitter fabric can be used to create special effects. The head and hands are stuffed with a high-density cotton to maintain shape and form while the clown is in its compressed state in the box. The jester's hat is best left hollow. It has just the right "floppy look" and gives an extra inch of length to the clown's height.

Slip the clown over the spring and close the lid. If the spring forces the lid open, squeeze the spring with pliers to remove some of its springiness. Continue to adjust until the weight of the lid is enough to keep the clown down. Attach a kitchen cabinet clamp to the inside of the box and the underside of the lid to increase resistance, if desired.

FINISHING

The thin woods used in the jack-in-the-box are best rubbed with a small amount of furniture oil to give a lustrous look to the wood. Continued oiling and wiping are necessary to bring the wood to its maximum luster. Repeat the oiling and wiping process for one week on a daily basis. Repeat once a week for a month for best effects.

Warmed carnauba wax can be applied with a clean cloth to give the box a pleasant finish. After the wax is buffed for an hour, let it stand for the night. Repeat several times, changing cloths each time. Practically all surfaces can be oiled or waxed with no difficulty.

Figure III–54.
Puppet poised in the box and detail of spring mechanism inserted in puppet head and attached to base.

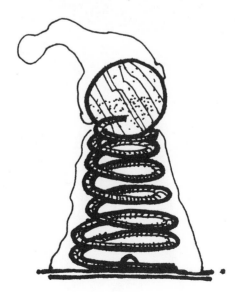

Truck With Bobbing Heads

Figure III–55.
Truck With Bobbing Heads.

As the wheels turn, heads move up and down as if riding over bumpy terrain.

TOOLS
Handsaw
Hacksaw
Hand drill
¼-inch drill bit
¾-inch flat-spade bit
Half-round file
Mallet
Pliers
Paint and paintbrush
Pencil and paper

MATERIALS
Wood
  (Use a clear, light softwood.)
  Front cab: (2) 1 by 4 by 4 inches
              (2) 1 by 2 by 4 inches
              (1) 1 by 4 by 2 inches
              (2) 1 by 6 by 8 inches
              (2) 1 by 6 by 8 inches
              (1) 1 by 6 by 8 inches
  Faces: (3) round drawer pull knobs, 1 inch in diameter
  Wheels: (6) wood buttons, 1¼ inch in diameter or 6 pieces, ¼-inch thick, cut from a 1-inch-diameter dowel
  Headlights and axle mounts: assorted small pieces of wood
  Short body: (1) dowel, ½ inch in diameter by 3 inches
  Tall body: (1) dowel, ½ inch in diameter by 6 inches
2 pieces of coat hanger wire, 8 inches, for axles
Epoxy glue
Finishing materials *(See instructions.)*

THE TOY
The bobbing figures provide an element of surprise in these simply constructed boxes. This effect is accomplished with two bent axles that are attached to the dowel figures. As the wheels turn, the bent axles raise the dowels up and then just as quickly, down. Each axle, made of coat hanger wire, must freely revolve inside its own compartment. Epoxy glue is used to bond wheel to axle.

PROCEDURE
Construct the van and the cab frames as shown in the illustrations by butt-jointing the four sides together. Drill two ¾-inch-diameter holes in the top of each box. Enlarge the hole with a half-round file to enable the dowel to move up and down unhindered. Slip a metal axle through a predrilled 1/8-inch-diameter hole at the bottom of each dowel to be used for a body, at a point 1/8 inch up from the bottom. Drill axle mounts in the center with a 1/8-inch drill to accept coat hanger wire, and glue and clamp axle mounts to the bottom edge of each box. Turn each truck box over, and, with the needle-nosed pliers or slip-joint pliers, bend the axle to match the shape shown in the illustration. Apply epoxy cement to wheels (either button or dowel) and tips of wire axles and position wheels quickly for best bonding effect.

Paint the drawer knobs to make faces and lightly tap them onto the dowel ends with the mallet. Join both boxes together by applying wood glue to the front surface of the van and the rear surface of the cab. Clamp in place until dry.

Add headlights made from thin dowel discs of ¾-inch diameter. Glue top panels in place and clamp.

FINISHING

Spray-lacquer the entire toy to guard against denting of the soft wood and accidental contact with moisture. Three thin coats will suffice nicely for a durable finish. Lightly steel-wool to remove glossy surface if a dull finish is required.

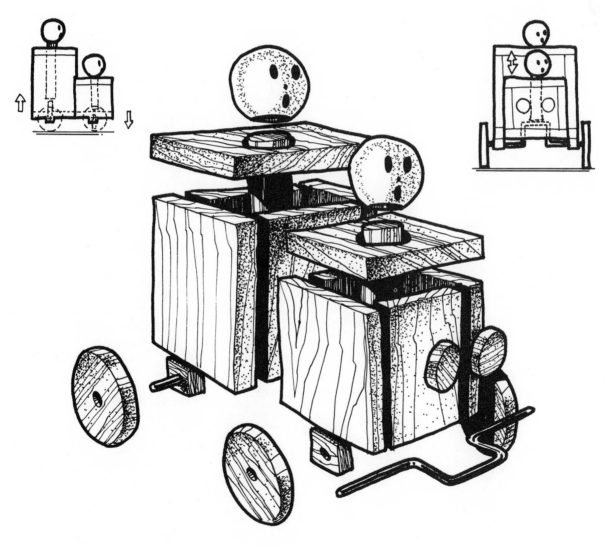

Figure III–56.
Exploded view of toy and front and side details showing motion of both figures.

Musical Trundle Toy

Figure III–57.
Musical Trundle Toy.

A musical wheeled object that plays a tune as it is pushed along.

TOOLS

Handsaw
Coping saw
Power drill or hand brace
¼-inch drill bit
½-inch drill bit
1-inch flat-spade bit
2-inch flat-spade bit
Keyhole file
Mallet (soft-head)
Clamps
Surform rasp file
Sandpaper, coarse, medium, and fine grades
Pencil and paper
Compass

MATERIALS

Wood
   (Use oak—red oak or white oak—for all pieces.
   Cut handle connectors from dowels.)
   Frame: (7) 1 by 3 by 18 inches
          (2) 1 by 3 by 12 inches
          (1) 1 by 2 by 12 inches
          (1) 1 by 6 by 14 inches
   Key brace bar: (1) 1 by 1 by 12 inches
   Handles: (2) 1 by 2 by 20 inches
   Trip Hammers: (5) 1 by 1 by 12 inches
   Keys: (5) 1 by 1 by 8 inches
   Revolving Bars: (5) 1 by 1 by 3 inches
   Wheels: (4) to be cut from 4 pieces of wood, each
          8 by 8 by 1 inch
   Handle bar: (1) 2 inches in diameter by 18 inches
   Trip hammer pegs: (5) ½ inch in diameter by 1½
          inches
   Axles: (2) ¾ inch in diameter by 17 inches
   Box-frame handle connector: (1) ½ inch in dia-
          meter by 16 inches
Carpenter's hide glue
Finishing materials *(See instructions.)*

THE TOY

During the eighteenth and nineteenth centuries, the trundle toy was one of the most useful inventions in that it helped the child learning to walk. The youngster pushed the toy ahead of him, and it served as a balance rod. An early seventeenth-century woodcut depicts a child pushing an animal ahead by means of a stick, perhaps suggesting the more popular version that was soon to be invented and widely used. The toy reached its apex as a training aid in the nineteenth century when trundle toys had ingenious devices built in to amuse the child as they walked and pushed. Bells, chimes, grating sounds, and vibrational clanking noises were emitted as the toy was put to its test.

The one illustrated here is a more substantial version of the nineteenth-century trundle toy, assuming the proportions of a wagon rather than a small stick-and-cage trundle. The toy can only be pushed forward because the hammer, in reverse direction, locks under the bar. The top right illustration shows how each hammer (called a "trip hammer") rotates and strikes a block of short, medium, or long wood for a variety of sounds. The woods are of uneven length so as to produce different tones. The trip hammer is connected to the rear axle, which, when the wheel is in the forward mode, brings each hammer to a rising and falling position.

PROCEDURE

Dimension all pieces of wood to be cut on graph paper before actually sawing the oak. Transfer all measurements to the wood and cut pieces to size. Assemble the box frame by gluing two pieces of 1 by 3 by 12 inches to the two pieces of 1 by 3 by 18 inches. When dry, drill two ¾-inch-diameter holes in the two long sides of the box at points 1 inch up from the bottom edge and 2 inches in from each end. Enlarge the holes slightly by filing with the keyhole file until the axles turn freely. These will accept the axles for the wheels. Drill a ½-inch hole in both sides of the frame, 1 inch up from the bottom and 14 inches back from the front end of the frame. This is the dowel bar hole to be used to make the handle of the toy adjustable and hold the trip hammers.

Side-edge laminate five pieces of 1- by 3- by 18-inch wood to form a 1- by 15- by 18-inch rectangle. Trim to form the floor plate of the rectangular frame. Glue and clamp in place.

Inside the front of the box on the floor, glue and clamp one 12-inch-long, 1- by 1-inch bar, which is the brace for the five "keys," which are cut from 3 to 8 inches in length. The length determines the "pitch" of the note. Glue all five keys in place by allowing each end to be fastened to the top surface of the brace bar.

Push the rear axle through one side of the frame. The revolving bars, all of which measure 1- by 1- by 3 inches, have a ¾-inch hole drilled in the back and, in turn, are threaded onto the rear axle and glued in staggered positions. Be sure to glue the inside of each hole before threading. To keep the revolving bars in place, but not touching, a square block or spacer is placed in between each bar. The thickness of the spacers used between the revolving bars and corresponding trip hammers must be the same.

Round the two handle rails by means of the Surform rasp and drill two holes, ¾ inch in diameter, where they are to be connected to the box frame. The connection is made on the inside of the box by means of the ½-inch diameter by 15-inch long dowel.

Note that the front of each trip hammer has a small protruding dowel peg. These pegs are placed in ½-inch-diameter holes predrilled ½ inch deep and extend out by 1 inch. This gives the hammer the necessary right angle "head" to strike the key.

Push the handle connector dowel through one side of the frame. Slip one handle piece of the dowel followed by a spacer and a trip hammer. Continue threading hammers and spacers and finally, the second handle piece. The dowel is then pushed through the other side of the frame.

Slip the 2- by 18-inch dowel rod through the two upright handles and thoroughly sand all edges of the outer part of the toy.

The next step is to install the flat rear plate, with three 2-inch holes drilled at equal intervals, and the front plate. The holes in the rear plate allow the notes to escape. The faster the cart is pushed, the faster the tune is played. Glue the front and rear plates in place, clamp, and let dry.

Cut wheels from the 8-inch-square pieces of lumber. To do this mark the center of the square (where two diagonal lines intersect). Place the point of the compass at the center and the other leg at 4 inches. Rotate the compass to make a circle. Cut the wheels using a coping saw. Using the same center point, drill a ¾-inch-diameter hole in each wheel. Glue the wheels onto the axle ends. Use a waterproof resin glue in this instance to ensure a permanent bond.

FINISHING

Oak is a highly durable and weather-resistant wood. In the event that the trundle toy might be in contact with moisture, a spray- or brush-applied clear lacquer is to be used. All edges and areas that have coarse grain or rough surfaces should be sanded with fine sandpaper before any finishing materials are applied. A tack rag will remove small and unseen particles.

Figure III–58.
Exploded view of toy and detail of revolving bar striking trip hammer, which in turn strikes the key.

Pegged and Doweled Locomotive

Figure III–59.
Pegged and Doweled Locomotive.

An all-around toy made with assorted pieces of round stock, from a ¼-inch dowel to a baker's rolling pin.

TOOLS
Handsaw
Coping saw
Hand or power drill
Hand brace drill (for better leverage if power drill is unavailable)
¼-inch drill bit
½-inch drill bit
3/8-inch drill bit
¾-inch flat-spade or auger bit
Thin flat file
Adjustable wood clamps
Ruler
Pencil and paper

MATERIALS
Wood
(Use lightweight, light-colored softwoods. The wheels are cut from dowels.)
  Boiler: 6-inch-long sections taken from a baker's rolling pin
  Base: (1) 3 by 10 by 2 inches
  Cab: (4) 3 by 3 by 1 inch
  Wheels: (4) 2 inches in diameter by ¼ inch
    (4) 1 inch in diameter by ¼ inch
  Cattle guard: (1) 3 by 4 by 1 inch
Miscellaneous dowel pieces to be used for boiler stacks and inlay pieces around boiler, plus 2 small pieces of half-round molding to be placed on side of base.
Glue
Sandpaper, grades 120 and 220
Finishing materials (*See instructions.*)

THE TOY
This locomotive is based on the old switch engines and is essentially composed of three basic components—the boiler, the base, and the cab. The scale of the parts is up to you and should be worked out on paper prior to laying out the woods. The key to the design of the toy is that the scale must be kept relative to the other parts. Yet, exaggeration of the overall components is what gives a toy like this one its obvious character, because the prominent features are made all the more obvious and whimsical by their straightforward look and manner of construction. The dimensions given in the materials list are merely suggested sizes for your first one. Do not feel restricted to these measurements. Modify as you go along. I have found that following strict instructions in the making of a toy is a tedious and overly mechanical task. As long as suggested guidelines and basic proportions are observed, your creation will be just that—*your* creation!

PROCEDURE

These are the basic steps in the making of the locomotive. Think in terms of basic parts—the boiler, the cab, the base, and the wheels. Each has its own method of assembly. Once the basic parts have been completed with all their smaller pieces, then the entire unit is brought together to form an integral toy. Sand all pieces before assembly.

For the boiler, rolling pins are not expensive, so, if possible, obtain a new one or one that is only slightly used. This is important because in contrast with the finer woods you will be incorporating in this toy, a worn rolling pin will pale. Cut away a 6-inch section of the pin. Clamp it to the worktable by means of adjustable wood clamps at both ends of the round stock. Using the ¾-inch flat-spade bit, bore three holes all the way through the stock. The holes are spaced about every 1 inch. Drill a smaller hole with the ½-inch drill, on both sides of all three holes to a depth of ½ inch. In turn, rotate the stock and drill four even rows of holes to a depth of ½ inch, using the ¼-drill. Plug these smaller holes with corresponding dowel pegs and allow the dowels to rise above the surface of the pin by ¼ inch. The medium-sized holes are treated in the same manner, but in this instance the dowels rise above the barrel by ½ inch. The large holes, which go all the way through the barrel, have two purposes. They serve not only to hold the smokestack, but also to connect the boiler to the middle section. Before inserting the large dowel rods through the smokestack holes, proceed to make the base, cab, and wheels.

The shape of the base is a simple one. From the 3- by 10- by 2-inch hardwood stock, notch out the axle supports with the coping saw. To create the space between the two axle supports, cut away a square block of wood to match the opening pictured in the illustrations. Saw into the wood to a depth of 1 inch along the side of one axle support. Continue cutting at a right angle to this first cut by turning the saw 90 degrees. Proceed slowly to prevent snapping the blade. Cut across 2¼ inches to the inside of the opposing axle support and repeat the 90-degree turn.

Continue down 1 inch until wood is cut away. If necessary, file the 90-degree angles until smooth, using a thin, flat file. On the wide surface of the base section, toward the front, bore three holes of ¾-inch diameter to correspond to the dowel rods that will connect the boiler to the base. The depth of each bore should be ¼ inch. Drill an axle hole in each axle support, using the ¼-inch drill bit. Attach two small pieces of half-round molding toward the front edge of the base section to form side rails.

The cow catcher is 1 inch thick and tapers to a blunt point. It is also notched to form an axle mount in both forward and rear sections. At a point 1 inch in from back edge of the stock, cut in ½ inch and across ½ inch, and then out at an angle of 45 degrees. Cut the back edge to the desired shape. Bore ¼-inch holes all the way through to accept the axles. Glue and clamp the cow catcher to the middle section after all holes have been drilled.

Illustrated are two versions of the cab. The exploded view depicts a more complex cab based on multi-shaped pieces that, when assembled, essentially form the same cab as in the other drawing, where the cab is made by notching a block of wood and attaching the roof. Choose the one that suits your design, piece, and then glue and clamp the cab together.

Before installing axles and wheels, check to see if axles turn freely. If not, sand axles before gluing. Glue wheels in place. Attach boiler assembly to the base by means of the three large dowels. (The suggested length of the dowels is 5½ inches to 6 inches. If the rolling pin is 3 inches in diameter, the dowels will rise above the boiler by approximately 2½ inches.) Apply a thin bead of glue on the underside of the boiler where it contacts the base. If the dowels make a firm and snug connection between boiler and base, no clamping should be necessary. Position the cab assembly on the aft section of the base and glue in position. Use two rubber bands to tighten the cab to the flat wood surface.

Examine the engine when the glue has cured. Any small fittings that need attention can be glued and sanded in turn.

FINISHING

The initial sanding of wood prior to its assembly obviates the need for extensive sanding once the toy is completed. Glue spills and remaining rough wood are sanded by applying sandpaper around a thin piece of wood or finger and lightly stroking the problem area. Fingernail rasp boards come in handy for the hard-to-reach areas.

A wide range of finishes are available for sealing and oiling the toy. Oils, because of their penetrating effects, are helpful and easily flow into the tight spots and crevices. They also tend to darken the wood and need continual rubbing to bring out the full color. If wax is used, it should be warmed to the consistency of a syrupy liquid and lightly brushed on the wood's surface, then buffed with a soft rag. Clear lacquers, shellac, varnishes, and polyurethane finishes can be applied by means of an aerosol can, stiff brush, or a spray unit. If propellants are used, several thin coats are better than one or two thick coats.

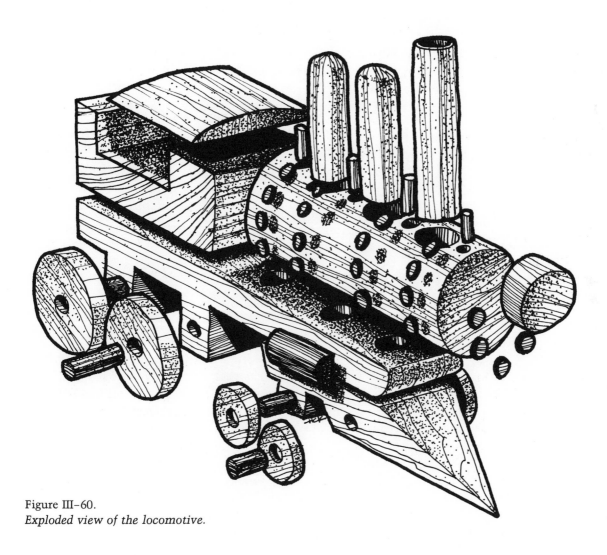

Figure III–60.
Exploded view of the locomotive.

Suppliers of Wood and Woodworking Tools

WOOD

Robert Albrecht
8635 Yolanda Avenue
Northridge, California 91324

American Hardwood Company
1900 East 15th Street
Los Angeles, California 90021

Craftsman Wood Service
2729 South Mary Street
Chicago, Illinois 60608

Crowe & Coulter
Box 484 CP
Cherokee, North Carolina 28719

Curtis Woodcraft Supply Company
344 Grandview
Memphis, Tennessee 38111

House of Hardwood
2143 Pontius Avenue
West Los Angeles, California 90025

R & R Hardwood
2520 West Hellman Avenue
Alhambra, California 91803

Reel Lumber Service
P.O. Box 879
Anaheim, California 92805

Sculpture House
38 East 30th Street
New York, New York 10016

Simmons Hardwood Lumber Company
1150 Mines Avenue
Montebello, California 90640

TOOLS

Adjustable Clamp Company
417 North Ashland Avenue
Chicago, Illinois 60622

American Machine and Tool Company
Fourth Avenue and Spring Street
Royesford, Pennsylvania 19468

Arco Products Corporation
110 West Sheffield Avenue
Graslewood, New Jersey 07631

Black & Decker Manufacturing Company
Towson, Maryland 21204

Brookstone Company
Petersborough, New Hampshire 03458

Buck & Hickman
Head Office
100 Queen Street
Sheffield S1 2DW, England

Craftsman Wood Service
2729 South Mary Street
Chicago, Illinois 60608

Curtis Woodcraft Supply Company
344 Grandview
Memphis, Tennessee 38111

The Cutting Edge
295 South Robertson Boulevard
Beverly Hills, California 90211

E. C. Emmerich
Fabrik Erstklassiger Werkzeuge
563 Remscheid - Hasten 14, Herderstr, 7.
Postf. 140152, West Germany

Frank Mittermeier, Incorporated
3577 East Tremont Avenue
Bronx, New York 10016

Skil Corporation
5033 North Elston Avenue
Chicago, Illinois 60630

Stanley Tools Limited
600 Myrtle Street
New Britain, Connecticut 06050

Garrett Wade Company, Incorporated
303 Fifth Avenue
New York, New York 10001

Woodcraft Supply Corporation
313 Montvale Avenue
Woburn, Massachusetts 01801

Glossary of Common Woodworking Terms

Across the grain: In a direction at or nearly at right angles to the grain of the wood.

Bevel: The sloping edge of a work piece.

Bit: The working part of a drill, available in assorted sizes and configurations.

Burr: The rough, furry edge produced by cutting or boring.

Check: A crack, split, or fissure in the surface of the wood.

Chuck: The tool or bit holder on a lathe, brace, or drill.

Countersink: To chamfer around or widen the upper portion of a bored hole in order to allow a head of a screw or nail to come level with the wood's surface.

Dado: A groove worked with or across the grain.

Dimensioning: Bringing wood down to the required size. Also, to mark paper or stock with measurements.

Dowel: A round wood rod.

End grain: Ends of wood fibers exposed after the cut has been made.

Face side: Principle surface of the wood.

Heartwood: The hard portion of the tree trunk close to the center.

Inlay: Ornament composed of shaped pieces of thin contrasting wood set into the surface of the primary piece.

Jaws: The holding member of a tool.

Kerf: The path cut through wood by a saw blade.

Miter: A kind of joint in which two pieces of wood join each other to form a 90 degree angle with the angle of the miter at 45 degrees.

Paring: The thin shaving of wood removed by a tool such as a gouge or chisel.

Rabbet: A stepped cut made at the edge of a board so that another piece can be fitted to make a joint.

Sapwood: The wood layer just under the bark of the tree, which often varies in color and texture from the inner heartwood.

Scribing: Making an incised line on stock by means of a sharp instrument for purposes of measuring or to serve as a guideline for cutting.

Shank: The stem or straight part of a tool nearest the handle.

Shim: A thin strip of metal or wood used to pack material usually for tighter fit.

Stock: Synonomous with wood to be used for cutting or otherwise worked.

Springwood: The softer wood layers in the tree-ring pattern grown during spring or wet weather.

Stop cuts: Cuts made vertically in a surface to outline or provide protection against accidental splitting while removing excess wood.

Strike: To make short hammering motions with a mallet against a tool.

Summerwood: The harder wood layers of the tree-ring pattern grown during summer or dry seasons.

Undercut: To cut back beneath an exposed edge.

Bibliography

Culff, Robert. *The World of Toys*. London: Hamlyn Publishing Group, 1969.

Daiken, Leslie. *Children's Toys Throughout The Ages*. London: Batsford Ltd., 1968.

Edlin, Herbert L. *What Wood Is That?* New York: Viking Press, 1969.

Fritzsch, Karl. *An Illustrated History of Toys*. London: Abbey Library, 1965.

Jackson, Albert and Day, David. *Tools and How To Use Them*. New York: Knopf, 1978.

Jackson, Nevill. *Toys Of Other Days*. London: Benjamin Blom, 1968.

Johnstone, James B. *Woodcarving*. California: Lane Publishing Co., 1971.

Lapidus, Saul. ed. *Wood, Metal and Plastic*. New York: David McKay, 1978.

Meilach, Dona Z. *Creating Small Wood Objects*. New York: Crown Publishing, 1976.

Paz, Octavio, and The World Crafts Council. *In Praise of Hands*. New York: New York Graphic Society, 1974.

Schiffer, Herbert and Nancy. *Woods We Live With*. Pennsylvania: Schiffer Ltd., 1978.

Schuler, Stanley. *The Illustrated Encyclopedia of Carpentry and Wood Working Tools, Terms and Materials*. New York: Random House, 1973.

Simon & Schuster. *The International Book of Wood*. New York: Simon & Schuster, 1976.

Studley, Vance. *Making Artist's Tools*. New York: Van Nostrand Reinhold, 1979.

U. S. Department of Agriculture. *Wood Handbook*. Washington D.C.: United States Government Printing Office, 1976.

Metric Conversion Table

Linear Measure

1 inch = 1,000 millimeters = 2.54 centimeters
12 inches = 1 foot = 0.3048 meter
3 feet = 1 yard = 0.9144 meter

Square Measure

1 square inch = 6.452 square centimeters
144 square inches = 1 square foot = 929.03 square centimeters
9 square feet = 1 square yard = 0.8361 square meter

Liquid Measure

1 fluid ounce = 0.0296 liter
1 pint = 0.4732 liter
1 quart = 0.9464 liter
1 gallon = 3.7854 liters

INDEX